Before He Was Buddha

Before He Was Buddha

The Life of Siddhartha

Hammalawa Saddhatissa

INTRODUCTION BY
Jack Kornfield

Seastone

BERKELEY, CALIFORNIA

Published by:
Seastone, an imprint of Ulysses Press
P.O. Box 3440
Berkeley, CA 94703-3440
www.ulyssespress.com

Credits: Published by arrangement with the Sri Saddhatissa Buddhist Center. Sidebar
quotes by Buddha and Buddhist masters are from *Buddha's Little Instruction Book* by Jack
Kornfield. Copyright © 1994 by Jack Kornfield. Used by permission of Bantam Books,
a division of Bantam Doubleday Dell Publishing Group, Inc. Parts of this book were
previously published as *The Life of the Buddha*, Harper & Row. Photo credits appear on
page 129.

Printed in Canada by Transcontinental Printing

10 9 8 7 6 5 4 3 2 1

Editorial and production staff: Leslie Henriques, Ray Riegert,
    Steven Zah Schwartz, Aaron Newey, Lily Chou
Design: Leslie Henriques, Sarah Levin
Cover art: *The Buddha*, Odilon Redon (1840-1916), French,
    Palace of Tokyo, Paris/SuperStock Fine Arts

The Library of Congress has cataloged the hardback version as follows:

Library of Congress Cataloging-in-Publication Data
    Saddhatissa, H.
        Before he was Buddha : the life of Siddhartha /
    by Hammalawa Saddhatissa
        ; introduction by Jack Kornfield.
                p. cm.
        Includes bibliographical references.
        ISBN 1-56975-136-6 (cloth)
            1. Gautama Buddha. I. Title.
    BQ882.S213 1998
    294.3'63
    [B]--dc21   97-50454
                                                            CIP

Paperback ISBN: 1-56975-230-3

Distributed in the United States by Publishers Group West, in Canada by Raincoast
Books, and in Great Britain and Europe by Airlift Book Company

Table of Contents

Introduction
by Jack Kornfield

Y ou hold in your hands a treasure, one of the most beloved stories of the human race, told and retold over the centuries. It is beloved because it reminds us of the possibility of freedom, of awakening the heart. It is repeated because it is our story; together with the Buddha each of us can remember our own ignorance and struggles and each can sense the path we, too, might follow to live a life of freedom in thought, word and deed.

It is an honor to introduce Venerable Saddhatissa's sensitive and human retelling of the Buddha's life story. In the time of this account, 2500 years ago, it was excitedly whispered from town to town when the Buddha was coming. It was considered a marvel to see an Awakened One and hear his teachings.

More marvelous, this ancient and wise understanding has lasted and is still with us. We now have the teachings of the Buddha translated into nearly every language, and in the past generation they have spread throughout the world. Today there are hundreds of thousands of Buddhist monks and nuns, and hundreds of millions follow this path of awakening.

The teachings of compassion and generosity, of quieting the mind and opening the heart are as relevant today as they were in the community around the Buddha. They have been carried like a lamp for each new generation to illuminate the universal questions of human suffering and find our own Buddha Nature in response.

Central to this story of the Buddha's journey is the account of the four sights or heavenly messengers that shocked the young Siddhartha with the truth of human frailty and suffering. In leaving the protection of the palace, the Prince first encountered an old person, then one who was grievously sick. Next he saw a dead body and finally an ascetic renunciate seeking a solution to human suffering. Perhaps we can each remember the powerful encounter when we first saw someone grievously ill, or saw our first corpse, and the effect such first-hand knowledge of death has had in our life.

For the young Prince, these four sights turned him to the search for liberation, to seek the deathless. And while the first three messengers are to be seen all around us, the fourth has not, until now, been a part of the Western landscape. In the years since the first publication of Venerable Saddhatissa's book, even that has changed. Let me tell one story of how this is so.

In 1978, my teacher, the renowned forest master Ajahn Chah, brought his senior Western monk the Venerable Sumedho to London to begin one of the first Buddhist monasteries in the West. The temple offered to them was a small apartment in London, which, being simple monks, they accepted. Ajahn Chah insisted his monks go out in the early morning, as usual, with their alms bowls so that all who wished might offer food. When certain Western devotees suggested that no one would understand, Ajahn Chah asked how else would Westerners learn but by seeing monks, even if it took a hundred years.

So Venerable Sumedho went out mindfully and barefoot each morning, though he rarely received any food. One morning, however, while walking with his bowl through a nearby London park, he was stopped by an older man who asked what he was doing. Venerable Sumedho explained that he was a monk out on alms rounds—he was actually a forest monk who usually meditated in the woods as had the Buddha, but in England they had been offered a city apartment, so they were out on the London streets to allow anyone to make offerings. The man was delighted to meet a forest monk, saying he had a beautiful forest in one of the most elegant parts of England and had been looking for a way to preserve it. So after some conversation, there in the park the man placed in the monk's bowl an offering of this forest, which has now become one of the major Buddhist monasteries of the West.

Nearly twenty years later the monks at several monasteries do receive food as they walk through the English countryside. But since the beginning, it was not for alms food alone that monks were told to go out each day. "You must remember," said Ajahn Chah, "that as a monk you are one of the heavenly messengers, the sight of which prompted the Buddha to go forth on his quest for enlightenment. It is your duty to go forth daily for the benefit of all. Who knows who will see you. The sight of a saffron-robed renunciate can be the inspiration for the next Buddha to go forth."

In this spirit, this new edition of Buddha's biography is a timely event. To read the Buddha's story is again to be invited to see the truth of life and awaken. Every day brings us the messengers. And every day we can remember that in their midst, goodness of conduct and freedom of heart is only a moment, a breath away.

Take pleasure in this story, read it slowly, digest it, reflect upon it. Let it be a blessing and a mirror for your own heart. And in this mirror, may it lead you to relinquish greed, hatred and delusion, may it lead you to live wisely and follow the Noble Path. In this way, the Buddha assures us, "The earth will not be free of enlightened beings."

Blessings,
Jack Kornfield
Spirit Rock Center
Woodacre, California
1998

ONE

The Golden Child

In the sixth century before Christ in the foothills of the Himalayas near the present-day border between India and Nepal there was a small but prosperous kingdom ruled by the warrior people Sakya. The capital city of this kingdom was Kapilavastu, and the land around was thickly dotted with smaller towns and villages. To the south of this kingdom lay the country of Kosala, and beyond that the kingdom of Magadha, in the area of the modern Indian state of Bihar around Rajgir. To the east lay the land of Koliya, from which came Queen Mahamaya, the wife of the Sakyan ruler, King Suddhodana.

In the year 560 BC there was great excitement in the land of the Sakyans because Queen Mahamaya was to bear a child. According to the custom of the time a woman expecting a baby would return to her parents'

home for the birth, and in due course it was arranged for Queen Mahamaya to make the journey to the neighboring kingdom of her father. The King sent soldiers ahead to prepare the way and the Queen set out, carried in a decorated palanquin and attended by a large company of guards and retainers.

On the way to Koliya the party passed by a garden called Lumbini Park where, attracted by the trees and flowers, the Queen ordered a halt. It was intended to be only a rest, but while the Queen was lying in the leafy and fragrant shade of a Sala tree in full blossom she went into labor and gave birth to a son.

There was no longer any reason to continue the journey to Koliya and the party returned to Kapilavastu, where the new prince was greeted with great rejoicing. He was named Siddhartha, which means "wish fulfilled," by a proud and doting father.

Such, in outline, is the account given in the Pali scriptures of how the man who was to become revered by millions throughout most of recorded history as the Enlightened One, the Perfect Being, the Buddha, made his entry into the world. The date of his birth—the full moon day of the month of Vesak, corresponding to May in our calendar—is very sacred, for in Buddhist tradition it is the date not only of the Buddha's birth but also of his Enlightenment and death. And, indeed, the account of this nativity, like so much else written down about the Buddha's life, especially the early years, is full of legendary and symbolic elements. It would be impossible to disentangle the purely historical events from their fantastic and miraculous embroidery, but it would in any case be an exercise of little value; the essential features of the Buddha's life and teaching are quite clear, and of the rest, if many incidents did not happen as reported, they might as well have done, such is their symbolic quality.

Before continuing with the account of the Buddha's life, something must be said about the historical circumstances. At this period, two and a half thousand years ago, the civilization that had grown up in northern India following the settlement there of Aryan invaders from Central Asia was already quite complex and sophisticated. The term Hindu did not exist at that time—it was coined much later—but the chief elements of what was to become known as Hindu society were well established. The most obvious of these was the organization of the community according to caste. The variety of castes in India is bewildering, but traditionally they have all fallen into one of four groups—at the top the Brahmins, who had the right to act as priests and were the custodians of religious knowledge; next Kshatriyas, or warriors, who generally provided the ruling class and were responsible for governing and protecting the community; then the Vaishyas, or merchants, who kept the economic life of the community going; and finally the Sudras, who did most of the hard work as artisans, laborers and servants.

The family into which the Buddha was born belonged to the Kshatriya clan Gautama. But though the Kshatriyas formed the nobility and governing class of society, the spiritual leadership was held by the Brahmins (hence the name Brahminism—the religious system of the time). Kings relied on Brahmins not only to perform religious functions but also to give advice and guidance. So, not surprisingly, priests figured prominently in the early life of the Buddha as the proud King Suddhodana thought about the career of his son and sought clues to his destiny.

One of the first visitors to the King after the birth of his son was a venerable sage named Kala Devala (also called Asita). Kala Devala was renowned for his wisdom and his reputed powers of clairvoyance, and it was he who first suggested, when he came to the palace to pay his respects to the new prince, that King Suddhodana's son was to be a man out of the ordinary. On seeing

Siddhartha he first smiled and then began to weep. Alarmed, Suddhodana said: "Why are you weeping? Is any misfortune likely to come to the baby?" "No," replied Kala Devala. "I smiled because I have been privileged to see a being who, I perceive from certain particular signs, is surely destined to become a fully enlightened one, a Buddha. But when I look into my own future I see that I shall not live to hear him deliver his teaching. That is why the tears came to my eyes. Rejoice, King, for the son that is born to you will become the greatest being in the whole world."

> *"If you wish to know the divine, feel the wind on your face and the warm sun on your hand."*

The concept of enlightenment was well known among religious devotees of the time and, as the career of the Buddha shows, many strove after it by way of the hermit's asceticism or the monk's discipline. The term "Buddha" itself, meaning "wise one," was not uncommonly applied to holy men of acknowledged spiritual stature. But the idea of a royal prince abandoning his heritage in favor of a life of austerity was not as easily accepted, especially among members of his family who would have other ambitions for him. Suddhodana therefore began to be worried.

The method of fortunetelling by which Kala Devala had arrived at his prediction was to "read" a person's body for certain marks or characteristics indicating the future course of his life—a kind of whole-body palmistry. In order to test Kala Devala's interpretation the King summoned eight of the most learned Brahmins in the land to him who were also adept in body-reading.

Seven of the Brahmins, after studying the child, concluded that there were two possible courses open to him. If he decided to remain in the world he would become a great emperor. If, on the other hand, he decided to give up the world and seek enlightenment he would become a Buddha. But the eighth Brahmin, Kondanna, was unequivocal. "His markings show that his future can go in only one way," he told the King. "A time will come when he will witness four special signs and as a result he will renounce the world and go out to seek enlightenment. Eventually he will achieve that enlightenment and become a Buddha." So impressed was Kondanna by what he had read in the child's appearance that he himself decided then and there to renounce the world and, accompanied by four friends of like mind, went away to wait for Siddhartha to grow up and attain Buddhahood. Kondanna and his group later featured prominently in the Buddha's career.

King Suddhodana was greatly upset by this prediction, and it was to obsess him as his son grew up. But meanwhile the child was the focus of everyone's admiration. His skin, it is said, had a golden hue and gleamed with a metallic glow. His eyes were blue "like the flower of the flax plant," his hair was black with a bluish tinge and his limbs were perfectly molded.

On the seventh day after his birth Siddhartha's mother, Queen Mahamaya, died. He was not deprived of motherly care, however, for the queen's sister, Prajapati, took responsibility for him. Polygamy was common among the nobility of that society, and Prajapati was also married to Suddhodana. According to the texts, she herself gave birth to a child on the day that Mahamaya died, but she put out her own son to be looked after by a nurse and brought up Siddhartha as her own, with all the love of a real mother.

After a few years Siddhartha was sent to school, where he joined the children of other noble families. His ability quickly impressed his teachers and he rapidly learned a wide range of subjects, including languages and mathematics. He also became proficient in sports like wrestling and archery. He excelled in all things, surpassing his fellow pupils, and even going beyond what his teachers could teach him. He was tall, strong and handsome, and his good manners and kindness endeared him to everyone.

Every year in the land of the Sakyans a ploughing festival was held. It seems to have been a largely ceremonial affair, suggesting a fertility ritual. The King himself drove the first pair of bullocks, which wore golden trappings on their horns and pulled a golden plough; other nobles of the kingdom drove bullocks wearing silver harnessing and drawing silver ploughs. When Siddhartha was seven the King took him to the ploughing festival. During the proceedings the boy was taken by his attendants to rest under a rose-apple tree on a specially prepared couch. While seated there he forgot all about the ploughing festival and fell into meditation, breathing in the measured and controlled way of skilled practitioners, until he entered a trance. It was the first mystical experience recorded in his life. It was in this way that his attendants found him when they came back a little later, aloof from his surroundings, in a state of rapture. Time had stood still for him, and as if to make this point the accounts say that the shadow of the rose-apple tree under which he was sitting had not moved from the time the attendants left him up to their return. This event was reported to the King who came hurrying to witness this latest evidence of his son's uniqueness.

"If you can't find the truth right where you are, where else do you think you can find it?"

Much is made in the accounts of Siddhartha's early life of his compassion for living things. One day he was walking in the woods with his cousin Devadatta, who later, when the Buddhist community had become established, was to take on the role of a troublemaker. Devadatta was carrying a bow and arrows with him, and seeing a swan fly past overhead he took aim and shot it. Both boys ran quickly to where the bird had fallen, and Siddhartha arrived first. The swan was still alive, so Siddhartha gently drew the arrow out of its wing. He then took some leaves and squeezed the juice from them onto the wound to stop the bleeding and tried to calm the frightened bird. When Devadatta arrived and wanted to claim the swan Siddhartha refused. "If you had killed it, it would have been yours," he said. "But it is only wounded, and since it is I who have saved its life it belongs to me." The argument went on until Siddhartha suggested putting the case before the court of wise men. After hearing all the evidence their verdict was: "A life must belong to the one who tries to save it. A life cannot be claimed by one who is only trying to destroy it. Siddhartha has the right to take the wounded swan."

Meanwhile, King Suddhodana continued to ponder the prophecies made by the Brahmins at his son's birth, and as the boy grew up he worried particularly about Kondanna's prediction that Siddhartha would renounce the world after seeing four special signs. So one day he sent again for his Brahmins—only seven this time, since Kondanna had disappeared to await the transformation of Siddhartha into a Buddha—and asked them to explain what was meant by the four signs. Unlike Kondanna, the seven Brahmins had allowed two possible courses for Siddhartha's life; he would become either a Buddha or a great emperor. He would opt for the former if he were to be confronted in turn by four men of different conditions—an old man, a sick man, a dead man and finally an ascetic, one who had renounced the world to seek deliverance from suffering. Well, thought the King, I must ensure that my son does not see any such signs. Immediately he ordered that no old or sick people and no sign of death should be permitted near the prince. Guards were specially posted to enforce this. No ascetic was allowed within a mile of him. He was given young servants, and any mention of illness, old age, death or monasticism was strictly forbidden. Even fading flowers and leaves were removed from gardens and pleasure parks so that the prince should not see anything that might suggest decay and death.

At the same time all possible luxuries and delights were provided for Siddhartha. Three palaces were built for him, one for each season of the year in that tropical region—the hot season, the rains and the cool months of winter. Extensive parks and hunting grounds, decorated with ponds full of fish, water lilies and swans, were prepared.

In this environment Siddhartha developed into a young man of great strength and beauty, and also of outstanding intellectual ability. He outstripped all his contemporaries in the martial arts, while in knowledge and agility of mind he surpassed even the most renowned pundits.

In due course, King Suddhodana decided the time had come for him to marry, and one day he summoned all the eligible girls in the kingdom to the palace for Siddhartha to make his choice. Among them was his cousin Yasodhara, a beautiful and charming girl. Siddhartha's choice fell on her, to the King's great pleasure, and they were married with much ceremony and rejoicing. By the time that Siddhartha was nearing his twenty-ninth birthday Yasodhara was expecting a baby, and King Suddhodana had begun to think that everything was, after all, turning out as he wished.

But though denied evidence of the human condition, and provided with every possible comfort and diversion, Siddhartha remained thoughtful and preoccupied. With the inevitability of a fairy-tale plot, the elaborate defenses erected by the King were soon to be eroded by reality, by the discovery, which was to become the basis of the Buddha's teaching, that life is suffering.

TWO

The Human Condition

All the diversions provided by King Suddhodana did not prevent the prince from feeling bored and restless, and one day he summoned his charioteer and personal attendant, Channa, to take him for a drive in the countryside. Channa chose four fine horses of the famed Sindhi breed, white and spotless like lotus blooms, and harnessed them to a magnificent chariot. Siddhartha took the reins, majestic and resplendent as a god.

They had not gone far before they saw standing in the roadway a hunched-up, tired-looking old man. At last the precautions taken by the King had failed. Siddhartha was astonished. "What is that?" he asked Channa, bringing the horses to a stop. "It looks like a man, but his hair is all white, he has no teeth, his cheeks are sunken, his skin is dry and wrinkled, and his eyes are bleary. Look at his bent back, his ribs protruding, his thin crooked arms and legs that seem as if they can hardly support his wretched frame, so that he has to lean on a stick. What kind of man is that?"

"That," replied Channa, apparently making little effort to sustain the elaborate structure of pretense that had shielded Siddhartha from reality up till then, "is an old man. It is someone who has been living for a long time, perhaps sixty, seventy or even eighty and more years, so that his body is worn out and decaying. It is nothing to be dismayed at, since it is a common thing. We all get old."

"Do you mean to say that we all of us become like that, that we all get old?" said Siddhartha. "That Yasodhara, and you, and all my youthful companions, and even I myself, must one day look like that?"

"Yes, my lord," answered Channa. "It is everyone's lot."

Siddhartha was so upset he could not go on with his drive. Instead, he turned the horses around and went back to the palace, deep in thought, too troubled to speak. When the King saw his son returning so soon after setting out he asked Channa the reason; and when he heard it he cried out in despair: "Now you have destroyed me." But the King was not one to give up so easily. In an effort to remove from Siddhartha's mind the memory of his meeting with the old man he ordered special dramas and amusements to be provided. He also doubled the guard around the palace grounds and reminded everyone of the strict instructions he had issued.

But once again Siddhartha decided to go for a chariot ride with Channa, and on this occasion they encountered a man who was ill. He was so weak he could not stand up, but rolled and writhed on the ground. His eyes were bloodshot, his mouth was frothing and he groaned and beat his breast in agony. As before Channa explained the phenomena and once more Siddhartha was overcome with anxiety.

"Is this a rare thing, or does it happen to everybody?" he asked.

"Everybody is liable to get ill, my lord," replied Channa, then added by way of reassurance: "But if a man is careful about his diet, keeps clean and takes plenty of exercise he is likely to remain healthy. There is no need to worry."

"No need to worry!" exclaimed the prince. "First I see the horror of decay and old age, and now it seems everyone is liable to find himself in such a wretched plight as this man!"

As before they cut short their excursion and Siddhartha returned home with a heavy heart.

A third time Siddhartha and Channa set out and this time came upon a funeral procession. The mourners were wailing and beating their breasts, while, in contrast, the corpse they were carrying lay still and lifeless like a statue. Channa replied to Siddhartha's predictable questions and then went on: "Death, my lord, is the end of life. When life ceases, that is death. Your body dies when it can go on no longer because of old age and decay. Or else it dies because of disease. Breathing stops and the heart ceases to beat. But there is nothing strange about it. It is as common as birth, for everyone who lives must sooner or later die. There is nothing you can do about it, since it is in the nature of things, so there is no point in worrying about it. Just hope for a long life."

Siddhartha pondered this, and also the two earlier phenomena, and came to realize that these unpleasant facts that had been hidden from him for so long, thanks to the misguided concern of his father, represented the true nature of existence. Life was suffering. And then he began to wonder whether there was not some way out of this dilemma, some means of escape. "Must everyone I love, and I myself too, simply endure helplessly this tyranny of old age, disease and death?" he asked himself as they once more drove back to the palace.

Siddhartha and Channa went out a fourth and last time, and as before an unaccustomed sight awaited Siddhartha on the roadside. But this time it was not a scene of despair. It was a man with a shaven head, wearing an orange-colored robe that glowed with the mellow light of the morning sun, standing barefoot and holding a bowl in his hand. His face bore a calm, thoughtful expression and his gaze was directed downward, as if he was a person at peace, engrossed in pleasant thoughts. Halting his horses, Siddhartha asked Channa: "Who is this? Is it a man or is it indeed a god who stands there so calm and aloof, as if the sorrows and joys of this world do not touch him?"

"That, my lord," replied the dutiful Channa, "is an ascetic. It is a man who has seen how old age, disease and death afflict all beings, and has renounced the world to seek a solution to the enigma of life. He has no home, but shelters in caves and woods, begging enough food for one frugal meal a day and living a life of discipline and simplicity, striving to be pure in deed, word and thought and seeking deliverance from the world's suffering through meditation. He travels from place to place and tries to tell people how to live a good life and find happiness."

This was, of course, the fourth symbolic vision foretold by the Brahmins. Greatly impressed, Siddhartha did not turn back this time but instead drove on, deep in thought, until he reached the amusement park that had been the destination of all his excursions with Channa. In the park everything had been prepared for the prince's entertainment, with musicians, dancers, poets and scholars all waiting to attend him, and plenty of food and drink.

But Siddhartha would not be distracted from his train of thought and as he walked through the park so richly provided with possibilities of indulgence and diversion he thought to himself: "I must become like that ascetic. I too shall renounce the world, this very day, and seek that deliverance from suffering of which I have been unaware through all the years I have spent in superficial amusements."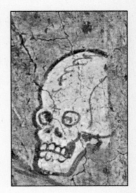

Eventually, tired of walking, he sat down in the shade of a tree. While he was resting, a messenger galloped up on a foaming steed with an announcement that should have delighted the young prince—his wife, Princess Yasodhara, had just given birth to a son. But far from feeling joy, Siddhartha greeted the news with dismay. "Another bond to tie me!" he exclaimed as he arose to return to the palace. But his resolve remained unshaken; nothing, not even the arrival of a son and heir, would now deflect him from the path he had chosen.

The King sensed the discontent in Siddhartha and, with the Brahmins' dreaded prophecy now fulfilled, privately resigned himself to losing his son. Nevertheless, in a last desperate attempt to hold him he arranged a grand feast and celebration to mark the new birth. The leading singers and musicians in the land were invited to perform.

The best and most beautiful dancers were summoned. The most sumptuous food was served. In deference to his father, Siddhartha attended the feast, but, preoccupied with his own thoughts, he took no interest in the lavish entertainment that had been laid out for his benefit, and as the evening wore on he began to doze off. In due course, seeing that they were performing for a sleeping prince, the musicians and dancers decided to have a rest as well, and soon they too were fast asleep. When Siddhartha woke up he was surprised to see all the people who had earlier been entertaining him lying around deep in slumber. And how changed they looked! Dancers and singers renowned throughout the land for their grace and beauty now sprawled inelegantly on the chairs and couches where they had laid down. Some were snoring loudly, others grinding their teeth like animals. The glamour of a short while before had turned to squalor. Siddhhartha's disgust with the worldly life was complete, and arising quietly so as not to disturb any of the sleeping bodies he called his attendant Channa and told him to saddle his favorite horse Kanthaka, in readiness for a long journey.

Before leaving he had one duty to perform. He had still not set eyes on the son whose arrival had coincided with his decision to renounce the world, so on his way out he paused at the room where the child and mother were sleeping. Yasodhara was holding the baby close to her, her hand covering the baby's face protectively. For a moment Siddhartha wrestled with an agonizing dilemma: if he moved his wife's hand to look at the child's face she might wake up and prevent him from leaving; but unless he did he would have to leave without seeing his son. He quickly made up his mind. "I must go without seeing my son's face," he said to himself. "But when I have found what I am now going out to seek I shall come back, and then I shall see him and his mother."

It was midnight as Siddhartha, accompanied by the faithful Channa, rode quietly out of Kapilavastu. Only when he had gone beyond the city gates did he pause to look back at the palace, now sleeping in the moonlight, where he had spent all his life and where he was leaving behind everyone he knew and loved.

Riding through the night, they came to the river Anoma, which marked the border between the Sakyan kingdom and the kingdom of Magadha. Once on the other side of the river Siddhartha dismounted. He then took off his fine silken clothes, handed them to Channa and told him to return with them and his horse to Kapilavastu. Such garments were not appropriate for an ascetic. Then he took out his sword and cut off his long hair.

Finally he put on some orange-colored robes, provided, according to legend, by a helpful deity, took up a begging bowl and dismissed Channa. Channa was loathe to go. "How can I go on living in the palace without you?" he said. "Let me follow you."

"No," replied Siddhartha. "Take my clothes and my jewelry back to my father and tell him and my mother and my wife that they must not worry. I am going away to seek an escape from the misery of aging, sickness and death. As soon as I have found it I will return to the palace and teach it to my father, my mother, my wife, my son and everybody else. Then everyone will be truly happy."

But it was Siddhartha's horse, Kanthaka, that figured in the poignant last moments of this parting, according to the story. When Channa eventually agreed to return Kanthaka refused to move. It was necessary for Siddhartha to talk to the animal before it could be persuaded to leave. But it had gone only a short distance when it stopped and looked around once more at its master. It required further persuasion from Channa to make it continue, and when it finally departed tears were rolling from its eyes. Later, it is said, the horse died of a broken heart.

THREE

Discovery

With all his worldly ties cut, and turning his back on the river Anoma, which now symbolically separated him from his past life, Siddhartha began the existence of a wandering ascetic. Such people were then, as ever since, common enough in India, and Siddhartha followed the usual practice of begging for his food and finding shelter wherever he could. People referred to him as a "holy man" or "ascetic," or, when they knew him well enough, by his family name Gautama. But no one suspected who he really was.

His identity first became known when he found himself in the city of Rajagaha, the capital of Magadha, and the site of the modern town of Rajgir in the Indian state of Bihar. Evidently his distinguished bearing caught the attention of the townspeople, for some of them remarked about it to the ruler of Magadha, King Bimbisara. "This young man, the ascetic Gautama as some people call him, is so charming and polite and well-groomed," they said, "that he does not seem at all like a mendicant."

> *"We do not need more knowledge but more wisdom. Wisdom comes from our own attention."*

On hearing the name "Gautama" the King realized this was the son of his friend and neighbor King Suddhodana, for the news of the prince's dramatic act of renunciation must have traveled fast. Immediately the King went out himself to look for Siddhartha, and as soon as he found him addressed him in a forthright manner. "What are you doing?" he demanded. "Why are you going about in this manner? Have you quarreled with your father?" He then implored Siddhartha to give up his ascetic life and even offered him half his kingdom if he would agree to do so and settle down in Magadha. But Siddhartha graciously declined, explaining his mission and his determination to go on searching for a happiness that was not dependent on the vicissitudes of life.

Meanwhile, the news that Siddhartha had set out on the spiritual road had reached the Brahmin Kondanna, the one who had originally predicted such a career for the prince, and he set out to join him. Kondanna lived with four other seekers of truth, Bhaddiya, Vappa, Mahanama and Assaji, and they went along with him. All six thereafter, clad in the orange robes of the ascetic, wandered around as a group.

The usual procedure, then as now, for anyone seeking spiritual enlightenment was to look for a teacher, or guru. Despite the strict ordering of society according to caste, and the numerous and detailed obligations that this entailed for every member of that society according to his status, the actual business of gaining and imparting religious knowledge was largely left to individual initiative. There were no officially recognized institutions of learning nor even a clear hierarchy of religious authority such as, for instance, the major Christian denominations possess. For spiritual guidance it was necessary to attach oneself to a teacher, an ascetic who by virtue of the experience and wisdom attributed to him had begun to attract and accept pupils. The authority of such teachers depended solely on their reputation.

There were many such teachers in India at that time, some of them with large followings. Often a teacher would be known for his attention to a particular aspect of religious discipline or for a particular doctrine, so that he and his group of pupils became an identifiable school, even perhaps a sect. It was up to the novice himself to decide to whom he would become attached. In accordance with this practice, the first major step taken by Gautama and his companions was to choose a guru.

One of the most celebrated teachers in that part of India at that time was Alara Kalama, whose system was devoted to achieving a level of meditation that, such is the inadequacy of language, is described in the texts merely as a "state of Nothingness." It was under Alara that Gautama and his companions first enrolled. Gautama studied especially hard. Indeed, he made such progress that one day Alara announced he could teach him no more.

"You are equal to me now," he told Gautama. "Will you stay here and help me teach my pupils?"

But Gautama was not satisfied. "Is that all you can teach me?" he replied. "Can you not teach me how to escape from death, illness and old age?"

"No," said Alara. "I cannot teach you something I do not know myself. No one in the world knows that."

So Gautama and his friends left. As they wandered around the country they passed onto others what they had learned under Alara, but meanwhile they looked about for a teacher who could take them further. In due course they came across another renowned teacher Uddaka Ramaputta, who headed a school dedicated to cultivating an advanced form of mental concentration termed—again rather unhelpfully for the uninitiated—"neither perception nor nonperception." This was something that had reputedly been achieved by the founder of this school, Rama, but even Uddaka himself, to whom Rama had relinquished charge of his pupils before he died, was still striving toward that goal. Under Uddaka's supervision Gautama was successful, whereupon Uddaka with due humility invited him to become the leader of the school. But again Gautama felt unsatisfied, and once more departed to continue his search.

The little party eventually arrived at a place called Uruvela, and here they decided to settle for a while. It was a good spot for their purpose—a tranquil wooded area, with a river at hand to provide water and a village nearby where they could beg for their food. They set up a hermitage, and resolved to try and find their own way, unaided by any teacher, to their spiritual goal.

Mortification of the body has been practiced by many people in many places as a spiritual discipline, and this was the procedure that Gautama, along with his companions, now decided to follow. He began by eating less. At first he restricted himself to one meal a day, then gradually it became a meal every two days, then every three. He no longer begged but fed himself on a rude diet of fruit, roots and the leaves of certain plants. His once healthy, robust body became emaciated. His skin became dry and wrinkled, and his eyes sank into their sockets until, as the text graphically puts it, they resembled stones in a deep well. He began to suffer terrible pain and hunger.

But his self-torture did not end there. He punished his body by holding his breath for long periods, until his head would seem about to burst. In the hottest season he would stay out in the burning sun during the day and indoors, where the air was oppressively stuffy, at night. In winter he would bathe in icy water. To demonstrate his contempt for his body he took to wearing the filthiest rags salvaged from rubbish heaps or even from corpses awaiting cremation. He also put his mental endurance to the test. On the nights of the new moon and full moon, an awesome time when supernatural beings were abroad, he would go and sit alone in mortuary grounds. Nor did the more obvious threat from marauding wild animals in such places scare him away.

And all the while he practiced meditation, though to little avail.

For six years Gautama underwent this regime before he decided it was leading him nowhere. Then one day he collapsed. He was found by a shepherd who gave him milk and took him into his care. He did not leave the shepherd until he had regained some of his old health and robustness, and then he went to rejoin his five companions. They, meanwhile, were continuing to practice their austerities, and when they saw that Gautama was no longer doing so they were shocked and upset. In fact, they were so disgusted at what must have seemed to them a failure of discipline, if not actually a betrayal of the undertaking, they jointly agreed that they would have no more to do with him. They got up and departed, leaving him behind. But Gautama, now left to himself, went on building up his strength until, it is said, his body regained its original golden hue and the thirty-two physical features indicating that he was destined to become a Buddha were once more clearly visible.

There lived in the neighborhood at that time a woman called Sujata, the daughter of a wealthy property owner. Sujata was expecting a baby and she had vowed that if a son was born to her she would make a special food offering to the deity of a nearby banyan tree. The banyan tree, with its characteristic aerial roots that grow into trunks and thus enable the tree to spread and renew itself, has long been regarded with particular reverence in India

and must have been from quite an early stage the focus of animist cults. Sujata duly bore a son and set about the elaborate ritual of preparing a meal fit for a god. First she milked a hundred cows, and fed this milk to fifty of them. She then fed the milk of these fifty cows to twenty-five of them and so went on with this process of concentration, known as "working in the milk," until she was left with the milk of only eight cows. With this rich and highly nutritious milk she made a rice preparation, using a special cooking vessel, and taking care that not a drop was allowed to boil over or go to waste. Finally she emptied the preparation into a golden bowl, filling it to the brim. She then sent her maid to the banyan tree to make arrangements.

Meanwhile, Gautama had chanced upon this banyan tree and had sat down under it to meditate. When the maid approached she was astonished to see this golden-hued figure, radiating a kind of luster, sitting motionless at the foot of the tree. She rushed back to her mistress to announce excitedly that the deity himself had appeared in order to accept the offering. Sujata duly came hurrying with her bowl of milk rice, appropriately draped with a fine silken covering, and was likewise struck by the seated figure glowing golden in the morning sun. Less credulous than her maid, perhaps, but overcome with awe, Sujata made her offering to Gautama, addressing him as follows: "Venerable Sir, whoever you may be, god or human, please accept this milk rice, and may you achieve the goal to which you aspire."

Sujata then placed the offering in Gautama's hands, saluted him reverently and withdrew, giving no thought to the precious bowl she had left with him.

The time had indeed come for Gautama to achieve what he had been seeking for so many years, and the events of that day, as described in the texts, are imbued not only with symbolic meaning but with peculiar calm and dignity. Taking the offering, he went to the nearby river Neranjara, and putting the bowl on the bank he entered the water to bathe himself. He then returned to the bank, sat down with the bowl in his lap and began his last meal as an aspirant to Buddhahood. The meal over, he washed his hands and the bowl and placed the bowl on the water to float. Then he said: "If today I am to attain full enlightenment, may this golden bowl swim upstream." The bowl immediately did so. Gautama spent the rest of the day relaxing in the woodland along the river bank.

In the evening Gautama got up and made his way to the Bodhi tree—the "Ficus Religiosa," another tree sacred in India and known as the "Tree of Enlightenment"—which he had chosen as the place for his great act of meditation. On the way he met the grass cutter Sotthiya who gave him some bundles of "kusa" grass. This grass was regarded as sacred and was used by Brahmins for sitting on. Gautama spread this grass at the foot of the Bodhi tree, turned to face the East and sat down in a meditating posture. Thus began the great trance from which he was to emerge on the full moon day of the month of Vesak as a Fully Enlightened One, a Buddha.

The course of Gautama's meditation is elaborately recounted in the ancient texts. At an early stage he was confronted with worldly temptations in the form of demons—an episode markedly similar to the temptations of Jesus in the wilderness. He then moved through various stages of spiritual ecstasy, called to mind all his previous forms of existence, and pondered how things come into being and disappear. With his mind purified, he then considered the nature of defilement, how it is caused and how it can be destroyed. In so doing he shed from his mind the various forms of defilement—the defilement of sensual desire, of the wish for continued existence, of delusion—and finally achieved the deliverance that he had sought for so long. "Now the cycle of rebirth is ended for me," he said afterward, when talking about his experience. "For me this world no longer matters."

> *"Those who are awake live in a state of constant amazement."*

According to one account Gautama spent seven days in this trance, emerging as the sun was rising and the full moon of Vesak was setting. Then he spent further periods of time in the vicinity of the Bodhi tree, gazing at it with gratitude for having sheltered him and walking up and down in front of it. Many other events, laden with symbolic significance, are said to have taken place during this period.

Soon after Gautama attained Enlightenment, two merchants, Tapussu and Bhalluka, came by. Seeing Gautama seated under the Bodhi tree, they prepared a meal for him of flour and honey and offered it to him. After eating the food the Buddha talked to them about his experience and the two merchants became his first lay disciples, the first Buddhists. Gautama was now aged thirty-five.

FOUR

The Middle Path

The Buddha was now ready to begin his mission, and he asked himself to whom he should first expound the Doctrine, who would most quickly understand. His mind turned to his former teacher, Alara Kalama, a learned and wise man already far advanced in his progress toward spiritual perfection. Alas, he had died. Then he thought of Uddaka, the disciple of Rama. But he, too, was dead. Finally he remembered the five companions with whom he had shared a rigorous asceticism before breaking away to seek enlightenment alone. They were still at the deer park of Isipatana near Benares, about a hundred miles away, and he set out to make the long journey.

After many days of traveling—on foot, of course— he arrived one evening at the deer park. Surprised, no doubt, to see him approaching, the five had not forgotten the scorn and resentment they had felt on parting from him. So as he walked toward them they remarked sarcastically to one another: "Look, here comes that so-called ascetic Gautama, the luxury-loving fellow who could not keep up a life of austerity and fell back into ease and comfort. Let's ignore him. Don't show him any respect or offer to take his bowl or his spare robe from him. Let him come and sit down if he wants to, but he's not worth bothering about."

As the Buddha came closer, however, they began to see that he had somehow changed. He had a majestic, authoritative air about him such as they had not seen before, and without their realizing it their hostility evaporated. Soon they were going forward to greet him, and while one respectfully took his bowl and robe another prepared a place for him to sit and a third hurried off to fetch water to wash his feet.

That evening he delivered his first sermon. It is known as "The Turning of the Wheel of Truth" and it is an occasion that holds an important place in Buddhist lore. The first to grasp the full significance of the Buddha's message was Kondanna who had originally predicted Siddhartha's enlightenment, and as he did so the Buddha exclaimed: "Kondanna has realized it! Kondanna has realized it!" The full exposition of the Doctrine, however, evidently lasted well beyond that evening for the Buddha later described how two of the monks would go out begging while he instructed the other three, and vice versa, until all had fully absorbed his teaching.

This is perhaps an appropriate place to set out the main elements of this teaching. In its classical form the Buddha's Doctrine is expressed in dry, methodical, almost mechanical terms. Each aspect is neatly subdivided and categorized in such a way that it might have been laid out as a chart. And that is indeed what it is meant to be. At a time when there was little literature most learning was transmitted orally from teacher to pupil in a way that was easy to memorize. Thus we have as the core of Buddhist Doctrine the Noble Eightfold Path, the Four Noble Truths, the Five Groups of Clinging and so on. These are a convenient way of organizing complex and abstract concepts into a framework that is not only easily memorized but ensures the transmission and preservation intact of the essential features of the teaching. And these are the terms in which the Buddha addressed the five who were to become the first disciples of Buddhism.

The basis of the Buddha's philosophy is the Four Noble Truths. The first three of these are really stages of a simple logical argument that parallels the Buddha's own early progress from the comfortable life of a prince to the search for enlightenment. The argument goes as follows:

(1) life is full of suffering—a "vale of tears"—because of illness, aging, discontent and the awareness of death; (2) the cause of this suffering is desire, or attachment to the world in such a way as to become liable to suffering—i.e. desire for sensual pleasure, desire to see an end to unpleasantness, desire to go on living, etc.; (3) therefore, the way to eliminate suffering is to eliminate desire.

The fourth Noble Truth reveals the way to achieve this removal of desire; and that way is the central part of the Buddhist discipline: the Noble Eightfold Path, or the Middle Path. Explaining this the Buddha told his five disciples: "There are two extremes that should be avoided by a man who renounces the world. One of these is the practice of those things related to the passions, and particularly sensuality; this is low, uncivilized, unworthy and unprofitable, and is fit only for the worldly minded. The other extreme is the practice of self-mortification, which is painful, undignified and equally unprofitable." Both of these extremes, of course, were familiar to the Buddha. The sensual life was the one he had followed as a young man, while it was his abandonment of rigorous asceticism that had so offended those who were now listening to him. He rejected the former because it retarded one's spiritual progress and the latter because it weakened one's intellect.

The alternative was the Noble Eightfold Path, a form of conduct that avoided both self-indulgence and

self-mortification. The eight requirements of this discipline are generally labeled as follows: Right Understanding, Right Thought, Right Speech, Right Action, Right Livelihood, Right Effort, Right Mindfulness and Right Concentration. They require a little explanation.

Right Understanding means seeing life as it is, realizing the nature of existence as summed up in the Four Noble Truths. This is subdivided into twelve items representing various aspects of this understanding.

Right Thought means a pure mind, the avoidance of feelings that obstruct progress to perfection, such as lust, malice and cruelty. Right Thought is closely linked to Right Understanding, Right Effort and Right Mindfulness.

Right Speech means cultivating the same characteristics in one's words as in one's thoughts. One should refrain from telling lies, backbiting, idle gossip and the like, and address people in a kindly and tolerant manner. Correct speech should not be loud, excited or opinionated; it should also avoid inflaming the passions of others, as may happen when addressing crowds in the open air, so Right

Speech may not be easily achieved by politicians and demagogues.

Right Action is broken down into five precepts, each covering negative and positive behavior. The first of these "five commandments" prohibits killing and urges charity and kindness to all living things. The other precepts deal with theft and generosity; sensuality; sincerity and honesty; and the use of intoxicating drink or drugs. Among these, two tend to be stressed particularly: abstaining from taking life and from sensual indulgence. But all five injuctions are important for the disciple aspiring to higher things. Right Action is also allied to other steps on the Eightfold Path, notably Right Understanding, Right Effort and Right Mindfulness.

Right Livelihood is straightforward: in earning your living you should not engage in any business or activity that conflicts with or compromises the conduct of life according to the Buddha. It follows that any kind of deceit or exploitation, anything that causes harm or injustice to others is to be avoided. Five forms of trade in particular are prohibited: these are trade in arms, in living beings, in flesh, in intoxicating drinks and in poison. But the occupations of soldier, hunter and fisherman are also excluded, as are usury, prostitution and soothsaying. One has to live, of course. But since the Buddhist ideal is a life of homelessness and freedom from material attachments, one's needs should be as simple as possible, even where there are family and business responsibilities. With Right Livelihood are associated Right Understanding, Right Effort and Right Mindfulness.

Right Effort consists of fostering noble qualities and rejecting ignoble ones. It is divided into four parts, constituting a moral training by which the other obligations of the Eightfold Path can be fulfilled. By practicing this training the Buddhist will achieve what are known as the Ten Perfections: generosity, moral integrity, renunciation, wisdom, energy, patience, honesty, determination, loving kindness and equanimity.

Right Mindfulness is the development of intellectual awareness in the service of spiritual progress. Here one is getting into the deeper levels of Buddhist philosophy, but in simple terms this means training one's mind to examine things in such a way as to recognize what is important and not to be led astray; it might be described as a kind of spiritual intuition. Four areas of experience are categorized for examination: one's body, one's feelings, one's mind and the ideas that arise in one's mind. With proper regard to these four Fundamentals of Mindfulness, one perfects the seven factors of Enlightenment, translated (inadequately) as: mindfulness, investigation of the Dharma (the essential teaching of the Buddha), energy, rapture, tranquillity, meditative concentration and equanimity.

Right Concentration is the final step of the path, the practice of meditation that leads to a full understanding of the impermanence of things and eventually to Nirvana. Meditation requires discipline and training like other activities. Steady, gentle breathing is recommended, while the mind tries to concentrate on tranquillity; whenever vagrant thoughts creep in they should be patiently expelled, and in the early stages at least devices like counting or repeating *formulas* can be employed to assist concentration. There are also five mental hindrances that need to be removed, or at least weakened, before meditation can really begin. These are: sensuality, ill will, laziness, worry and skepticism.

> *"To meditate is to listen with a receptive heart."*

The Buddha explained much else besides to his five companions. For instance he went into the doctrine of "no-soul"—an idea that, at least on the face of it, conflicts with many other religions and raises the question of whether Buddhism can strictly be called a religion at all. But the essentials are in the Noble Eightfold Path; as we shall see later, the Buddha himself did not favor philosophic argument for its own sake.

FIVE

The Community

Anyone who becomes a Buddhist monk becomes a member of the Sangha, the monastic Community or Order that lives and organizes itself according to the Discipline laid down by the Buddha. The Sangha grew rapidly following the conversion of the five ascetics. No doubt these, as veteran seekers after the Truth and old companions of Gautama himself, were already well on the way to conversion when the Buddha preached his first sermon to them in the deer park. What is striking about many of the subsequent conversions is that they were of people apparently without any particular predisposition to the holy life, often people who came in contact with the Buddha quite by chance while going about their ordinary affairs. There was nothing novel in those days about the idea of renouncing the pleasures of the world for a life of meditation, so the rapid spread of his teaching and growth of his following suggest his message must have had something unusually dynamic and arresting about it. No doubt much of the explanation lies in his persuasive and down-to-earth manner, and the numerous parables that appear in the course of his teaching certainly support this.

This intensity of the Buddha is illustrated in the very first recorded conversations he made after those of his five ascetic companions—in other words, the beginning of his mission in the world at large. One morning while the Buddha was sitting in the deer park near Benares, a young man named Yasa came by. Yasa appears to have been the epitome of the idle rich, a man bored with his wealth yet unable to see what else there might be in life. Upon hearing the Buddha explain his teaching, however, he quickly realized the futility of his career and asked then and there to become a monk.

Meanwhile, Yasa's parents had become alarmed at his disappearance and his father set out to look for him. Toward evening he came across the Buddha. The Buddha told him his son had become a monk and began to explain his teaching in such a way that the father resolved to become a lay supporter. He also invited the Buddha, together with his monks, now numbering six, to come to his house for a meal.

It was to become the custom for Buddhist monks after enjoying someone's hospitality to offer a discourse, known as "giving thanks," and this is presumably the first occasion on which this happened; for after the meal the Buddha talked about his teaching to those present, who included Yasa's mother, his wife (who in effect was now his ex-wife since he had cut his worldly ties) and fifty-four friends. These fifty-four were so impressed that they all asked to be accepted as monks. The Sangha had grown to sixty.

Later, it is recounted, when these men had achieved Enlightenment, the Buddha addressed them with these words: "Go forth, monks, and teach the truth, which is glorious in the beginning, the middle and the end, for the good of all beings. There are some whose eyes are not obscured by dust. Teach them, they will understand."

Like other religious teachers of the time, the Buddha was peripatetic, wandering from place to place teaching anyone who would listen. Throughout the forty-five years of his ministry he traveled widely in northern and eastern India, stopping only during the rainy season, when he and his monks would go into retreat.

His first journey took him by stages from the deer park to Uruvela. During this journey he went to sit down in a wood, where there also happened to be a group of people enjoying themselves on an outing. There were thirty men, each accompanied by his wife except one, who had brought along with him a prostitute. While no one was paying attention, this woman picked up the belongings of her companion and made off. Eventually the theft was noticed, whereupon everyone got up and started running about to try and find the woman. While they were busily searching they came upon the Buddha sitting under a tree, and asked him if he had seen a woman, explaining what had happened. The Buddha replied: "Which do you think is better: to try and find a woman or to discover yourselves?" Perhaps this reaction came as a surprise to them, but it seems they agreed it was more worthwhile to try and discover themselves, for they abandoned the search for the woman and sat down to hear the Buddha's words. In due course they became converted to his teaching and the men joined the Sangha.

At Uruvela were three famed holy men belonging to a religious sect whose members tied their hair in a certain way and were thus known as "matted hair ascetics." All three were called Kassapa; the most prominent, who had a following of 500 ascetics, was known as Kassapa of Uruvela, the others, who had followings of 300 and 200 respectively, as Kassapa of the River and Kassapa of Gaya. These men, with their followers, heard the Buddha and joined the Sangha, thereby not only greatly swelling its numbers at a still early stage but bringing to it their own prestige as holy men. This prestige seems to have been a factor in the conversion of another influential figure, a king, with all the consequences this must have had for the spread of the Buddha's teaching, at least in his territory.

This was King Bimbisara of the state of Magadha, the one who had earlier sought to dissuade Gautama from the religious life. In the course of his travels, the Buddha arrived with his now large number of followers at Rajagaha, capital of Magadha, and when King Bimbisara heard that the Buddha had come to his city he went to visit him, along with a large retinue. The King was struck by the fact that the renowned religious teacher Kassapa of Uruvela was now a follower of the Buddha. So were the Brahmins in the King's retinue, though apparently this was a cause of chagrin to them, perhaps because it dramatized the growing threat that Buddhism was making to the established Brahminical form of religion. But the Buddha proceeded in his usual fashion and addressed them along the following lines:

"Why are you unhappy? Because you are filled with wanting, with desire, to the point that eventually the desire becomes a thirst that cannot be satisfied even when you achieve what you desire. So how can you be happy? By ceasing to desire. Just as a fire dies down when no fuel is added, so your unhappiness will end when the fuel of desire is removed. You will find real happiness when you conquer selfish hopes and habits."

When the Buddha had finished speaking, King Bimbisara, together with his loyal retinue, asked to be accepted as lay disciples of the Buddha. Moreover, the King invited the Buddha and the Sangha to his palace, where he personally served them food and later dedicated his pleasure garden, the Bamboo Grove, to the Sangha for their use.

"Do not blindly believe what others say, even the Buddha. See for yourself what brings contentment, clarity and peace. That is the path for you to follow."

As mentioned earlier, the Buddha's practice was to spend each rainy season in retreat, or meditative seclusion, at one or other of a number of places he favored. The first such retreat was spent with his five original monks immediately after the first sermon. It was the seventh such retreat that saw the conversion of two men who were to become known as his chief disciples.

Near Rajagaha were the two villages of Upatissa and Kolita. The headmen of these villages were also known by these names respectively, and their two families were very close. One day Upatissa's wife, Sari, gave birth to a son; so did Kolita's wife, Moggali. Upatissa's son became known either as Upatissa or as Sariputta (Sari's son), while the son of Kolita was called Kolita, Moggaliputta (Moggali's son) or Moggallana.

From their earliest days these two boys were close friends and as they grew up they developed a common interest in drama. But they increasingly felt there must be more to life than what they saw on a stage and, one day, while watching a drama (it was called The Mountain Festival) they decided to leave home in search of the true meaning of life. They first went to a famous religious teacher named Sanjaya, who lived near Rajagaha. But he could not provide the answer they were seeking. So they made a vow that from then on they would each ponder and meditate as hard as they could in quest of truth and that whoever thought he had found it first would tell the other."

One morning while Upatissa was in the main street of Rajagaha he saw what appeared to be an ascetic going from door to door with a bowl begging for alms of food. But somehow this seemed no ordinary ascetic. Upatissa felt

there was an unusual modesty and calmness about him, and as he approached he was even more deeply impressed by the man's manner and appearance. There was a look about the man's face, he thought, of perfect peace, as of the smooth undisturbed surface of a lake under a calm clear sky. "Who can this be?" said Upatissa to himself. "Surely he must be one who has discovered what I am looking for, or else he is the pupil of such a person. I wonder who his teacher is. I shall follow him and find out."

So when the man had been to all the houses and was going out of the city gate, Upatissa went up to him and said: "Brother, your demeanor is so pleasant and your deportment so appealing, your face is so clear and bright. Please tell me who your teacher is, what is his name?"

The man was in fact Assaji, one of the five original monks, and he replied that his teacher was a great ascetic of the Sakya clan who had left his home and country behind in order to follow the homeless life and serve others.

Upatissa pressed him to explain the teaching he followed, to which Assagai modestly replied: "I am only a newcomer into the monk's life under the Buddha, so I do not know very much yet about his teachings. I cannot explain it to you in detail, but perhaps I can give you a summary of it in a few words."

At this, Assaji began to recite a verse that summed up the Buddha's doctrine of Causation. He had only spoken the first couple of lines, however, before Upatissa grasped the meaning and in great excitement he said to Assaji: "If this is the doctrine you have learned from your teacher then indeed you have found the state that is free from sorrow, free from death, something that has not been known to men for so many ages." Then he thanked Assaji, saluted him respectfully and went to tell his friend Kolita of his experience. Together they went to see the Buddha, were received into the Sangha and very soon became appointed his chief disciples. In Buddhist history they are accorded a special reverence—Upatissa as a monk of great wisdom and Kolita as one who developed miraculous powers.

SIX

Early Years of the Sangha

During the early years of the Sangha the Buddha and his monks lived wherever they could find a suitable spot—under trees, in caves or ravines, or even out in the open. The Buddhist monk, after all, dedicates himself to a life of homelessness. However, as the episode of King Bimbisara shows, it soon became common practice for wealthy people to dedicate gardens or other grounds to the Sangha for its use, and at quite an early stage the Sangha was given a roof of its own also.

The first few rainy seasons (after the original one near Benares) were spent in the Bamboo Grove given by King Bimbisara, and one day during one of these retreats a rich merchant of Rajagaha visited this park. Seeing the monks sheltering as best they could he offered to provide proper dwellings for them. They replied that the Buddha had not so far given any ruling on this question and they went to ask him. He agreed and, the story goes, the merchant had sixty houses built in the grove in a single day. The following day he invited the Buddha and his community for a meal at his place, at which time he formally presented the dwellings to the Sangha.

This act of generosity led to another, even more spectacular one. The merchant's sister was married to Anathapindaka, who happened to come to Rajagaha on business the day before the meal to which the monks had been invited. He arrived to find a tremendous bustle, with cooks making elaborate dishes and servants scurrying about preparing for what was obviously going to be a very important occasion. No one had time to pay the visitor much attention.

"This is strange," thought Anathapindaka, somewhat put out by his reception, "usually when I come here my brother-in-law drops everything in order to welcome me, but today he seems solely concerned with ordering his servants about and preparing for some big event. Can it be a betrothal that is being arranged? Or perhaps he has even invited King Bimbisara for a banquet?"

Eventually the merchant finished supervising the preparations and went to greet Anathapindaka. He also explained what all the activity was about and Anathapindaka was immediately curious. The next morning he went to the Bamboo Grove to meet the Buddha for himself. The Buddha was out walking and seeing Anathapindaka coming toward him he said simply: "Come, Sudatta." Surprised and delighted to be addressed by his first name, Anathapindaka prostrated himself at the Buddha's feet to receive instruction and in due course became a lay disciple.

Anathapindaka lived at a place called Savatthi, and he invited the Buddha to stay there during the rainy seasons; the Buddha agreed to this. On returning to Savatthi, Anathapindaka started to look around for somewhere to accommodate the Buddha and his followers and finally found the ideal spot—a pleasure garden belonging to a prince named Jeta. Jeta, however, demanded a high price— he would agree to sell the garden only for as many gold coins as would cover it like a carpet. There also followed a dispute as to whether Jeta had legally contracted to sell the park on those terms, but this was resolved and Anathapindaka had the gold brought to the park in cart loads. When all the coins had been spread over the park there was still a small space left uncovered near the gate. Anathapindaka told his men to get more coins but by this time Prince Jeta realized this was no ordinary transaction and he offered the remaining space as a gift. Later Jeta had a gatehouse built over the space, while inside Anathapindaka had dwellings and other amenities constructed for the use of the Sangha. This place became known as the Jetavana monastery, and was one of the main centers from which the Buddha operated.

Converts to the Buddha's teaching came from all backgrounds and circumstances. One of the most prestigious conversions in the eyes of people living at the time must have been that of a man named Upali. At the same time that the Buddha was traveling around northern India spreading his message, another great religious leader was busy establishing a faith that, like Buddhism, still flourishes, though on a much smaller scale. He was Mahavira, the founder of the Jain sect, which is probably best known for its strict adherence to the principle of avoiding harm to any living creature (orthodox Jains, for instance, wear a small piece of cloth over their mouths to prevent them from inadvertently breathing in insects). Upali was a prominent follower of Mahavira.

On one occasion when the Buddha was staying near Nalanda (later the site of a famous Buddhist university, the ruins of which can still be seen), Upali was among those who heard the Buddha speak. He was so attracted to the teachings that he said he would like to become a follower immediately. The prospect of winning such an adherent must have been highly exciting for the more politically minded Buddha's entourage. But the Buddha himself was not impressed by such considerations. Far from welcoming

Upali he cautioned him: "Think it over properly, Upali. A man of your distinction should not make hasty decisions." Upali, who does not seem to have been unduly modest about his status, was also surprised at this reaction, though it only served to confirm his intention. He replied to the Buddha: "If it had been any other religious group that I had asked to join they would have taken me through the streets in procession, boasting that such a celebrated man had renounced his creed in favor of theirs. But all you do is advise me to think it over!" He congratulated the Buddha on his frankness and thereupon joined the ranks of his followers.

"Spiritual life should include a great measure of common sense."

Another dramatic conversion was that of Punna, who later became a zealous missionary. Punna was a merchant from the island Sunaparanta (the location is not certain, though some scholars put it on the west coast of India) and once when the Buddha was staying at the Jetavana monastery at Savatthi, he came to the town with a caravan of goods to sell. While resting after a day's work he noticed that large numbers of people were going in the direction of the monastery; when he asked why he was told they were going to hear the Buddha. Having nothing better to do he went along too. It was an act of curiosity that was to change his life, for the effect of hearing one discourse by the Buddha was such that he handed over his money and the goods still to be sold to his brother-in-law, who was his business partner, and became ordained as a monk.

Later, after much spiritual practice, Punna felt he should go back to his home to propagate the Buddha's teaching there, and accordingly he asked the Buddha's permission. But the Buddha did not immediately agree; instead he tested Punna's resolution with a rather quaint catechism, which went as follows:

The Buddha: "Sunaparanta is inhabited by wild, barbarous tribes. They are wicked, fierce, violent and cruel. They are also given to abusing and annoying other people. If they abused and annoyed you, what would you feel?"

Punna: "I would feel that the people of Sunaparanta are good and gentle people, since at least they are not punching me or throwing dirt at me."

The Buddha: "But supposing they punched you or threw dirt at you, what would you feel then?"

Punna: "I would feel that they are good and gentle people, since at least they are not hitting me with clubs or weapons."

The Buddha: "But supposing they hit you with clubs or weapons?"

Punna: "Then I would feel they are good and gentle people, since at least they are not taking my life."

The Buddha: "But supposing they killed you, Punna, what would you feel then?"

Punna: "I would still think they are good and gentle people, for then they would be releasing me from this rotten carcass of my body. I should thank them for doing me a service."

At this the Buddha gave in to Punna's wish and sent him away with these affectionate words: "Punna, you are endowed with the greatest gentleness and forbearance. Go and live in Sunaparanta, go and teach them how to be free, as you yourself are free."

Gratefully, Punna took his leave and went back to his homeland. Before the end of his first rainy season there, we are told, he had gathered 500 disciples around him.

In contrast to such cases, many who joined the Sangha came from poor, unprivileged backgrounds. And no background could be poorer or less privileged than that of an outcaste.

One of the fundamental differences between Buddhism and the Brahminical religion in India at the time concerned caste. The organization of society into a structure of castes based on occupations began with the arrival of Aryan invaders from central Asia. As mentioned in the opening chapter, four broad groups of castes were established—Brahmins or priests, Kshatriyas or warriors (the group to which the Gautama family belonged),

Vaishyas or merchants and Sudras or menial workers. Outside the caste structure altogether were the outcasts, the untouchables, the lowest of the low. They lived outside the community, in ghettos of their own, their sole function being to dispose of the rubbish and waste of the community, and to remain inconspicuous. But this system was not merely a social structure, it was intimately bound up with the Brahminical religion, which regarded a man's caste as the reward or punishment for his karma in previous births. Each caste had its own function and obligations within society, but the untouchables were not recognized as a part of society at all. Theirs were the most degrading jobs—the disposal of sewage, street cleaning, the handling of animal carcasses—and they were expected to keep well out of the way of caste people, particularly Brahmins. Even today in India, there are orthodox Brahmins who consider themselves polluted if merely the shadow of an untouchable should fall on them. But Buddhism was from the beginning universal. The Buddha borrowed from Brahminism concepts such as karma and rebirth, giving different interpretations to them—but not caste. This, of course, was not to the liking of the Brahmins of the time, who no doubt saw the Buddha's ideas as dangerously subversive. The following story illustrates this.

While the Buddha was staying in Savatthi one of his personal attendants, Ananda (about whom more will be related in this chapter), went each day to the town to beg for alms of food. One day, on his way back to the community he saw a girl fetching water from a well, and asked her to give him a drink. The girl belonged to the lowest rung of untouchables, and aware of her contemptible status in the eyes of society she declined, saying that she was unworthy to give him water.

Ananda replied: "Sister, I am not asking about your family or your caste. I am not concerned with caste. But if you have some water, please give me some to drink." Whereupon the girl, whose name was Prakriti, gave him water and fell deeply in love with him.

The story goes on to tell how, with the aid of a magic love potion prepared by her mother, Prakriti tried to get Ananda to marry her. Ananda, though sorely tempted at one stage, was saved by the miraculous intervention of the Buddha. But Prakriti was not cured of her love, so the Buddha summoned her to him and while ostensibly sympathizing with her wish, instructed her in his teaching until she abandoned her feelings for Ananda and decided to join the Sangha as a nun. She became a very devout follower of the Buddha, with a thorough grasp of his teaching.

The news that the Buddha had ordained an untouchable girl, however, caused great alarm among the Brahmins and other leading citizens of Savatthi, and they protested to King Pasenadi about it. The King went to see the Buddha, along with an impressive entourage of Brahmins, warriors and others and asked him to explain his actions. The Buddha replied by telling a story about a man called Trishanku, an untouchable leader—perhaps the chieftain of a tribe regarded as outside the caste system. Trishanku had a son named Shardulakarna, who was highly learned, and with parental pride and ambition Trishanku decided to try and get his son married to the daughter of the distinguished Brahmin Pushkarasari. The Brahmin, of course, rejected the suggestion with disdain, whereupon Trishanku began to debate with him the whole validity of the caste system. He argued that there was no inherent difference between members of different castes in the way that there was between different species of animals or plants. Moreover, he sought to demonstrate that the link between caste and the doctrine of reincarnation and karma was a fallacious one. Eventually Pushkarasari was so impressed by Trishanku's arguments that he gave in and consented to the marriage. No doubt many of those hearing the Buddha tell the story were less easily convinced since the same line of reasoning is still being advanced today in the face of those who defend apartheid and

other modern forms of casteism. But at
least, it seems, the good citizens of Savatthi
did not make any further fuss about the
issue.

Another story concerns the untouchable Sunita, whose job was to scavenge the
streets. For this work he was paid barely
enough money to keep himself alive, and he
slept where he worked, by the roadside,
being unable to afford a proper shelter. He
also had to constantly be aware of contami-
nating any high caste person who happened
to come by because the penalty would
probably be a severe beating. So whenever
someone of a high caste approached he left
the road and stood at a safe distance away.

One day while he was busy sweeping a road, he saw
the Buddha approaching, together with a large retinue of
monks. Finding no place where he could hide himself in
time (he assumed these people to be caste-born holy
men, as indeed they mostly were) he did the next best
thing, flattening himself against a wall and folding his
hands in a gesture of respect. No doubt to his dismay,
the Buddha came straight up to him. But far from addressing him harshly, as he had expected, the Buddha
spoke in a friendly manner. Without beating around the

bush he asked Sunita if he would like to give up his job and follow him instead. Astonished and delighted, Sunita replied: "Sir, no one has ever spoken to me in a kind way before. Usually I am just ordered about. If you will accept a dirty, wretched scavenger like me, then of course I shall come with you and leave this filthy job." The Buddha ordained him then and there, and though he started as an ignorant, uneducated man, he later became a celebrated figure in the Sangha, enjoying the respect of great men.

SEVEN

Returning Home

Some time after the Buddha had begun his mission and his renown as a teacher had become widespread, his father, King Suddhodana, came to learn that he was staying at Rajagaha. One day he decided to send a messenger to the Buddha with an invitation to visit his home city of Kapilavastu and give his own people the benefit of his teaching—though we may suspect that what the King really wanted was simply to see his son again. The messenger arrived and met the Buddha, but before he could utter his invitation the Buddha let him hear his own message, with the result that the messenger quite forgot the purpose of his visit and joined the Sangha. Puzzled by the disappearance of his messenger the King sent another. The same thing happened, and so it did again until altogether nine messengers had been dispatched and lost. Eventually the King sent a childhood friend of Siddhartha named Kaludayi, and now the Buddha listened.

Accompanied by a large number of monks he set off for Kapilavastu and took up residence at a place prepared for them called the Banyan Monastery. It was seven years since he had left the city.

When word got around Kapilavastu people flocked to see this son of the soil who had become so famous. His own relatives began to speak of him in possessive terms as "our cousin," or "our nephew," and told their children "Go up to him and pay your respects." But the Buddha realized there was more local pride behind this welcome than genuine interest in his teaching; it would require effort and patience before the citizens would accept him for what he really was. According to one account he had to resort to the miraculous device of appearing suspended in the air in order to convince them; at that, it is said, everyone, including the King himself, prostrated themselves in reverence. However that may be, when the Buddha set out the next day with his begging bowl and started going from door to door the King was greatly upset. He went into the street himself and said to the Buddha: "Why are you disgracing me in this way? Why can you not have food in my palace? Is it right for you to beg your food in the very city where you once traveled about in splendor? How can you put me to shame like this?"

The Buddha replied that he did not mean to put the King to shame but that begging food was "our custom."

"What do you mean?" said the King. "Nobody in our family has ever had to beg. What do you mean 'our custom'?"

"Your Majesty," said the Buddha, "It is not the custom of your royal family. But it is the custom of true sages. Such people have always lived by receiving their food in this way."

Nevertheless, being a pragmatic man, the Buddha eventually gave in to the King's repeated appeals to have his food in the palace, and decided to try and convince his father of his teaching on the King's home ground. He was successful, for the King eventually became a devoted follower of the Buddha, his own son.

Despite the initial difficulty in persuading the people not to regard him merely as a local celebrity, the Buddha's visit to Kapilavastu greatly enriched the Sangha. Many of his kinsmen, including some of his closest relatives, became his followers during his stay there.

Prince Nanda was a stepbrother of Siddhartha and when he reached the age of thirty-five the aging King Suddhodana, no doubt until then hoping there might still be a possibility of his son returning to the kingdom, decided to give Prince Nanda Siddhartha's place in the palace. He also arranged for him to marry a princess, Janapada Kalyani, and prepared a separate palace for them to live in. All of these plans, the King decided, would be brought to fruition at a single big celebration, and when he knew that the Buddha had agreed to return to Kapilavastu he decided to hold the festival during his visit so that Nanda and Janapada Kalyani could receive his blessing.

The festival, of which the main event was to be the wedding of Nanda and Janapada Kalyani, took place on the third day after the Buddha's return, and the Buddha duly attended. After taking part in the wedding feast the Buddha blessed the couple and the rest of the gathering then departed. On his way out, perhaps because he was accustomed to have his begging bowl and other personal items carried by one of his followers, he handed his bowl to Nanda. Thinking this was a momentary aberration, Nanda said nothing until the Buddha started to disappear out of the palace, whereupon he gave chase, following the Buddha to the monastery. Janapada Kalyani, assuming her husband was going to see the Buddha off, urged him with the solicitude of a new bride not to be away for long.

> *"Some days we feel like strangers. When our heart opens, we will realize that we belong just here."*

But when Nanda arrived at the monastery to hand back the bowl he was met with a surprise. Instead of thanking him and letting him return to the wedding party, the Buddha asked him bluntly if he would like to become a monk. Such was his respect for the Buddha, who, it must be remembered, was also his elder brother and on that account alone entitled to be shown deference, that he could not bring himself to say no. So without further delay the Buddha got one of his chief disciples, Upatissa, to ordain him as a monk.

Perhaps understandably for a man who renounces the world on his wedding day, Nanda did not settle easily into the ascetic life. His mind was full of his beautiful abandoned bride, and he complained to his fellow monks that he was unhappy and homesick. He also showed a quite unmonastic concern about his appearance, using cosmetics in the manner of fashionable men of the time, and wearing neatly pressed robes. For his begging rounds he took not an ordinary bowl, but an elegant piece of glazed pottery.

When Nanda's unhappiness was reported by his fellow monks to the Buddha, the latter personally took him in hand. "Nanda," he said, "you are one of my clan who out of faith have forsaken the domestic life for one of homelessness. It is not right that you should wear carefully pressed robes, use cosmetics and carry a bowl of glazed pottery. You should be a forest dweller, one who eats only food given in alms, who wears robes made of discarded rags, and who lives without thought of sensual desire."

By dint of careful teaching the Buddha gradually weaned Nanda away from his worldly concerns, and in particular his yearning for his beautiful wife, so that he eventually became an exemplary disciple.

The other notable convert from among his family during this visit to Kapilavastu was his own son, Rahula, who was born at the time that Siddhartha left home in search of Enlightenment. Rahula, now aged seven, had been brought up by his mother, Yasodhara, and his grandfather, King Suddhodana. No doubt Yasodhara felt as bereaved by her husband's departure as the King, and when the Buddha returned to Kapilavastu, she decided to approach him through Rahula. Her ostensible concern, according to the accounts, was to secure for Rahula the inheritance that his father had abandoned, and no doubt this was indeed a preoccupation. But looking at the incident in a wider context, and particularly in view of Yasodhara's later history, one is tempted to see in it an element of forlorn longing for a husband who had not merely forsaken her but renounced all worldly attachments. At any rate, on the seventh day of the Buddha's visit Yasodhara dressed Rahula in fine clothes and took him to a place where the Buddha was having his meal. She pointed him out to Rahula and said: "Darling, do you know who that is?" Rahula replied in the matter-of-fact way of children: "That's the Buddha, mother." At this Yasodhara's eyes filled with tears, and she went on: "Darling, that holy man with the golden complexion, with all his disciples around him, is your father, and once he had great property. Go up to him and say: 'Father, I am a prince. When I become king I shall be a king of kings. Let me have my property, for what belongs to the father must belong to the son.'"

Rahula did as he was told, and approached the Buddha with the respectful, if somewhat ornate, greeting: "Father, I love even your shadow." The Buddha finished his meal and got up to leave, but Rahula followed him repeating what his mother had told him to say. The Buddha made no reply, nor did he attempt to discourage the child. But as he walked he thought: "He desires his father's wealth, but that is only a worldly thing, a source of trouble. I shall give him instead far greater wealth, the sevenfold noble wealth that I received at the foot of the Bodhi tree. Then he will be the possessor of an excellent inheritance."

"Good-humored patience is necessary with mischievous children and your own mind."

So when they reached the monastery, the Buddha asked one of his two chief disciples, Upatissa, to ordain Rahula a monk.

The news of this was a further shock to the long-suffering King Suddhodana, who went to the Buddha and respectfully but firmly urged him in future not to ordain children without the permission of their parents. "When you left home it made me very very sad," he said. "When Nanda left home I was also very unhappy, and my heart ached. Then I began to concentrate my love on Rahula, but now you have brought him here and ordained him as well."

The Buddha sympathized with this plea and thereafter no one was allowed to join the Sangha without the approval of his parents or guardian. Later this requirement of permission was extended to include the wives of intending members. Rahula nevertheless remained a monk and he features in one episode in which the Buddha teaches the importance of truthfulness. At the time Rahula was eleven, and the picturesque style of the Buddha's teaching suggests not just a holy man instructing a pupil but a kindly father giving guidance to his son. According to the text, the Buddha picked up a scoop used for pouring water and put a little water in it. Then he said to Rahula: "Rahula, do you see this drop of water in the scoop?"

Rahula replied with proper respect: "Yes, Sir."

"Well," said the Buddha, "people who tell lies have as much good in them as that."

Then the Buddha went on to say the same thing in different ways: first he threw out the water to demonstrate how untruthful people throw away their virtue, then he turned the scoop upside down to show how little regard they have for their virtue, and finally he compared them to the empty, hollow scoop itself.

The Buddha followed this with another metaphor. "Picture a royal elephant, Rahula, an elephant of high breeding, grown to its full stature, with tusks as long as the shafts of a chariot, and plenty of experience of war. In battle he performs well, using his legs and body properly, also his head and tusks and even his ears and tail. Yet he holds back with his trunk. His rider thinks: 'This elephant uses his limbs and body well, but he keeps his trunk back. He is not fully devoting himself to the service of the king.' But once he starts to use all his body, including his trunk, then his rider says: 'Ah, now he is devoting himself fully. He has no more need of training.' It is the same with people who are not wholly truthful, Rahula, until they are it cannot be said that they are devoting themselves fully. So, Rahula, you must discipline yourself never to speak an untruth, even jokingly."

The Buddha concluded his lesson with the question: "What do you think a mirror is for, Rahula?"

"To look at yourself in, Sir," replied Rahula.

"Right," said the Buddha. "And in just the same way you should constantly reflect upon the acts of your body, of your speech and of your mind."

Another of the Buddha's kinsmen to join the Sangha was the man who was to become perhaps the best-known and best-loved figure in Buddhist history—his cousin Ananda, who became his personal attendant.

EIGHT

Allies and Assassins

During the first twenty years of his ministry the Buddha had no regular attendant; various monks waited on him, performing tasks such as carrying his bowl or his spare robes. But a couple of incidents convinced the Buddha to have one regular personal attendant. One of these incidents is almost a comic moral tale. One day the Buddha was going on a journey accompanied by the monk Nagasamala, and when they arrived at a fork in the road they disagreed about which way they should proceed. Nagasamala, who was carrying the Buddha's bowl and robes, put them down on the ground and took the road of his choice, leaving the Buddha to pick up his belongings and go by the other one. Unfortunately for Nagasamala, he encountered some robbers who took his bowl and robes and hit him on the head. He rejoined the Buddha with a sore head and a heart full of remorse for his disobedience.

On another occasion the Buddha was accompanied by the monk Meghiya. As they passed by a mango grove Meghiya said he would like to stop and meditate for a while, and handed his bowl and robes to the Buddha. The Buddha did not think this was the time for Meghiya to meditate, but Meghiya insisted. After a while, however, he returned to the Buddha to admit that he had been unable to concentrate properly and that the interruption had been a waste of time.

This episode, incidentally, was an opportunity for the Buddha to define the factors necessary for the calm and concentration without which one cannot meditate. With his characteristic precision the Buddha identified five factors: (1) association with mature and spiritually developed people; (2) restraint of the senses; (3) the practice of Right Speech, keeping aloof from passion; (4) the practice of Right Effort; (5) insight into the nature of the First Noble Truth (i.e. that sorrow is a condition of life.)

No doubt as a busy teacher whose time was much in demand, the Buddha felt he needed a reliable and constant attendant and the above incidents merely illustrated that the practice he had followed for twenty years was not satisfactory. Besides, he was now aged over fifty-five. So during a stay at the Jetavana monastery he announced his intention to appoint a personal attendant. Both his chief disciples, Upatissa and Kolita, offered their services but the Buddha declined, saying the work they were doing was too valuable to be sacrificed in that way. Other leading monks came forward but were similarly rejected. Eventually the name of Ananda was suggested, though he modestly refused to push himself forward and waited for the Buddha himself to nominate him.

Ananda was the son of Amitodana, who was a younger brother of the Buddha's father, King Suddhodana. His name means "joy," and he was so named, it is said, because his birth was a source of great joy to his parents. He entered the order, along with other Sakyan princes, when the Buddha visited his home territory.

Ananda's devotion to the Buddha was total. From that time until the Buddha's death he was his constant servant, looking after his room, washing his bowl and robes, massaging his body and always keeping close to the Buddha in case he was needed. Later, the Buddha described Ananda as a learned, mindful, well-behaved and resolute disciple. Ananda is also famous for the part he played in the admission of women to Buddhist monasticism, an event dealt with later in this chapter. But partly because of his role in this controversial matter he came in for a great deal of criticism from some of his contemporaries and seems to have been treated as a scapegoat or focus for the grievances of some of his fellow monks.

So great, however, was Ananda's devotion, say the texts, that he never had enough time for meditation and so did not attain Enlightenment during the Buddha's lifetime. Only afterward did he do so, in time to take a leading part in the first convocation of 500 perfect saints who recited and memorized for posterity the teachings of the Buddha a few months after his death.

It may seem odd in the social climate of today, at least in the West, that the Buddha did not initially favor the admission of women to the Sangha. It is more easily understandable in the context of the society of his time, in which, as is still often the case in India, women had clearly defined obligations and responsibilities within the family and were not expected to want to go off alone in search of the spiritual life. Besides, to cut loose from their family would immediately expose them to dangers against which they were not considered able to defend themselves; so if the attitude of their menfolk was possessive it was also protective. The breaking down of this mental barrier was another event involving members of his own family.

Some time after the visit to Kapilavastu described above the Buddha returned for another stay. In the meantime, his father, King Suddhodana, had died, though not before achieving sainthood as a devout follower of his son's teachings. While the Buddha was staying in a place called Nigrodha's park, Suddhodana's widowed queen, Mahapajapati Gotami, who had brought up Siddhartha after the death of his own mother, came to see him and asked to be ordained into his community. The Buddha refused, and remained adamant when she asked a second and a third time. Mahapajapati went away sorrowful, and the Buddha moved to a place called Vesali where his community had a monastic lodging in a wood.

But Queen Mahapajapati was not easily put off and one day she arrived at Vesali, accompanied by some of her Sakyan kinswomen, to try again. To demonstrate her sincerity she had cut her hair off and was dressed in yellow cloth like the Buddha's disciples. She was standing at the entrance to the monastery when she was discovered by Ananda. He was surprised to see her and dismayed by her condition, because she was covered in dust, her feet were swollen from walking and she was sobbing miserably. Ananda asked her: "Gotami, what are you doing standing out here?" "Lord Ananda," she replied, "I am standing out here because the Buddha will not accept women for ordination." Ananda, moved by the sight of Mahapajapati, rushed off to see the Buddha, and immediately put to him the question of admitting women. The Buddha was adamant as before, so Ananda decided to apply the Buddha's own technique of logical persuasion in order to bring him around. "Supposing," said Ananda, "women were allowed to follow the

> *"If we could see the miracle of a single flower clearly, our whole life would change."*

religious life, would they be capable of achieving Enlightenment?" Without asserting that women were spiritually inferior the Buddha could not say so, so he replied: "They would, Ananda." Seizing his advantage, Ananda went on: "In that case surely it would be a good thing if women could receive ordination. And especially Mahapajapati Gotami, who nursed you and brought you up so devotedly after your own mother died." At this the Buddha gave in, though he stipulated a number of conditions for women ordinands, under which they must accept strict discipline and submission to the authority of monks. Mahapajapati thus became the first Buddhist nun, and in due course she was joined by other female members of the Sakyan clan, including Siddhartha's wife, Yasodhara.

In common with all groups and organizations once they have reached a certain stage of development, the Sangha became prey to politics and schismatic tendencies. The best known example of this is the episode of Devadatta, the Buddha's cousin and childhood companion.

Devadatta had joined the Sangha along with other Sakyans during the Buddha's visit to Kapilavastu, but it seems the rivalry, if not jealousy, that he had exhibited at the time of the dispute over the swan was not abated by maturity. On one occasion when the Buddha was visiting Kosambi, the territory of King Bimbisara, Devadatta decided to challenge the Buddha's leadership of the Sangha, suggesting that the Congregation of Monks should be turned over to his charge. The Buddha refused and issued a public proclamation denouncing Devadatta and dissociating the Sangha from his actions. Devadatta thereupon made an ally of King Bimbisara's son, Ajatasattu, who was becoming impatient for his father's crown, and suggested to him that each should assassinate the man who stood in his way. Ajatasattu duly got rid of his father and Devadatta prepared to do the same with the Buddha. Altogether, we are told, he made three attempts. First he hired assassins to kill him but they fell victim to the Buddha's persuasiveness and became converts instead. Then Devadatta climbed to the top of a mountain called the Vulture Peak and hurled a rock down on the Buddha as he passed below; but the rock only wounded the Buddha. Finally he dispatched an elephant to attack him, but like Daniel in the lions den, the Buddha used his moral power to subdue the animal's wrath.

The story of Devadatta's unsuccessful bid for leadership of the Sangha, like much else in the life of the Buddha, is threaded with strands of legend. But there are grounds for thinking there may also be an element of propaganda in the way he is pictured because, as his next step shows, he was the author of the first schism in Buddhist history.

Having failed to kill the Buddha, Devadatta went to him with a list of five demands. These in essence called for a strict, puritanical application of the Buddhist principles of homelessness and poverty, as well as vegetarianism. It may be that this was a cunning attempt to call the Buddha's bluff, or there may indeed have been some disquiet at the breadth of the Middle Way trodden by some of his followers. But as one who had spent years seeking the Truth through self-mortification the Buddha was alert to the danger of a cult of discipline and firmly rebuked Devadatta for his ideas.

Devadatta then broke with the Order and set up his own community with five hundred of the Buddha's followers, though these soon returned to the Sangha under the persuasion of the Buddha's two chief disciples, Kolita and Upatissa.

The story goes that toward the end of his life, when he had been suffering illness for some months, Devadatta repented and decided to make his peace with the Buddha. He had himself carried on a litter to the Jetavana monastery where the Buddha was staying, and, raising himself up, cried out: "I seek refuge in the Buddha." Thereupon the Buddha received him back into the Sangha, prophesying that he would eventually achieve Buddhahood.

There was jealousy, too, outside the community. The first conversions of untouchables had caused an outcry among the orthodox, and as the fame of the Buddha spread more and more, with people of both high and low estimate coming to honor him, so did disquiet grow among other religious leaders. Some of them went and appealed to the crowds: "Is the monk Gautama the only Buddha? What about us? We are also Buddhas! You should give us alms and show us honor in the same way." But this achieved little, and so subtler means were adopted that bore the characteristic stamp of political underhandedness as it has appeared in many places and at many times in history.

Two separate plots were hatched by opponents of the Buddha while he was staying at his Jetavana headquarters. The first revolved around a young woman of outstanding beauty named Chincha who had renounced the world for a life as a kind of wandering nun. For reasons that are not clear, Chincha felt herself under an obligation to a clique of the Buddha's opponents, and they saw in her a means of discrediting him. As for Chincha, despite having renounced the world, she was not lacking in worldly imagination, and once she was persuaded to cooperate in the plot, she carried out her part skillfully.

While the Buddha was in residence at the Jetavana monastery, it was common for people living in the nearby town of Savatthi to stroll out in the morning to offer him their greetings and again later in the day to hear him

preach, returning home in the evening. Dressed in a gaily
colored cloak, redolent of perfume and bearing garlands of
flowers in her hands, Chincha also started to make a daily
journey from Savatthi in the direction of Jetavana, though
in her case she set out in the evening and after spending
the night in a lodging provided by the plotters, returned
to the town the next morning. So each eve-
ning as she went out toward Jetavana she
passed the crowds making their way home
while each morning the procedure was
reversed. Naturally, this soon aroused curiosity, and people started to question her about
her conduct. At first she merely replied:
"What business is that of yours?" But after a few weeks
of this, by which time her travels had become well
known, she began to tell questioners: "I have spent the
night in a perfumed chamber alone with the monk
Gautama." As time went on she wrapped cloth around
her waist to make it appear she was pregnant, and started
openly saying the monk Gautama was responsible. Finally, when about nine months had elapsed, she tucked a
piece of wood under her cloak and went to Jetavana while
the Buddha was preaching. Staggering, as if exhausted by
her effort, she broke into his sermon and called out sarcastically in front of everyone: "Mighty monk, what a
mighty throng is here listening to you preach the Truth;

> *"Even loss
> and
> betrayal
> can bring us
> awakening."*

how sweet is your voice, how soft your lips. Yet you are the one by whom I have conceived a child, which is due at any time, and you have done nothing to help me prepare for it to be born." She went on some more in this vein and ended: "You know well enough how to take your pleasure, but you do not care to take responsibility for the child you have fathered."

The Buddha, who had been interrupted in the middle of his sermon, merely replied: "My sister, only you and I know whether what you say is true or false." At that moment a gust of wind blew her cloak open, and the piece of wood fell out, straight onto her feet. It must have been a hefty block of wood, for according to the story, it cut off her toes. Scandalized, the crowd rose up crying: "This hag is reviling the Buddha," and promptly drove her away, to the chagrin of the plotters, not to mention the toeless Chincha herself, and the greater honor of the Buddha.

Undaunted by this reversal, however, the monks hostile to the Buddha later made a similar though more elaborate attempt to discredit him. This time the principal figure was a woman named Sundari who, like Chincha, was of outstanding beauty and, like her, was persuaded to make it appear she was the Buddha's lover. But in her case events quickly took an unfortunate turn, for she had been playing her role for only a few days when the monks hired some ruffians to murder her and throw her body on a rubbish heap near where the Buddha was staying. On her disappearance the monks began to make a hue and cry and went to complain to the King, taking the opportunity to mention that she had lately been spending her nights at Jetavana. With the King's approval they organized a search and when her body was found on the rubbish heap they brought it ceremoniously into the town alleging to the King and the public at large that she had been killed by the Buddha's followers in order to cover up his affair with her. There ensued much public concern, but when this was reported to the Buddha he merely remarked: "Anyone who declares something has occurred when it has not must accept the sad consequences of his evil action." Meanwhile the King sent out his own men to investigate the incident. Before long they came upon the murderers, who were drinking with the proceeds of their work. They had started quarreling about the murder, and were hurling accusations at each other when the King's men found them, so they were immediately taken before the King where they confessed the whole thing. The King had the monks brought before him and ordered them to go through the city making a public confession of their crime before receiving due punishment as murderers.

NINE

Compassion and Common Sense

Expressed in the formal terms in which it has been recorded by the scriptures, the Buddha's teaching appears dry and forbidding. It comes to life in the stories we have of the Buddha's day-to-day activities as a teacher and leader of the Sangha and in his own parables. Here also we see something of his personality, serene but not remote, compassionate without being sentimental, intellectually subtle yet full of common sense. In his work he exemplified integrity of thought and action.

The starting point of Gautama's own search for Nirvana was the realization that sorrow is a condition of life, that one cannot avoid it, only rise above it, and this theme occurs frequently in the story of his career. One of the best known episodes on this theme is that of the bereaved mother and the mustard seed.

Kisagotami was a young woman from a well-to-do family who was married to a wealthy merchant in Savatthi. When their first-born child was about a year old he fell ill and died before a physician could be summoned. Kisagotami was beside herself with grief and began roaming the streets of Savatthi asking people if they knew of a medicine that would restore her child to life. Some people merely ignored her, others thought she had gone out of her mind and laughed at her, but no one could offer her any help. Finally she met a wise man who told her: "There is only one person in the world who can perform the miracle you ask. He is the Buddha, and at the moment he is staying at the Jetavana monastery. Go and ask him to help you." Kisagotami went to the Buddha and, placing the body of her child at his feet, told him her sad story.

The Buddha listened to her with patience and kindness and then said: "My sister, there is only one way to heal your affliction. Go down to the city and bring me back a mustard seed from any house in which there has never been a death."

Kisagotami felt a great elation and immediately set off for the city. She stopped at the first house she saw and said: "I have been told by the Buddha to fetch a mustard seed from a house that has never known death." "Alas," she was told, "many people have died in this house." She went to the next house and was told: "There have been countless deaths in our family." And so to a third house and a fourth until she had been through the city without being able to fulfill the Buddha's condition. Now she realized what the Buddha had intended for her to discover—that death comes to all. Reconciled to this sad reality she took the body of her child to the charnel ground for disposal and returned to the monastery.

"Have you brought the mustard seed?" asked the Buddha.

"No," she said, "nor shall I try to find it any longer. Now I understand the lesson you were trying to teach me. My grief had made me blind, and I thought that only I had suffered at the hands of death."

"So why have you come back here?" asked the Buddha.

"To ask you to teach me the truth," she replied.

Whereupon the Buddha began to instruct her, saying: "In all the world of men, and of the gods too, there is only one law—that all things are impermanent."

Kisagotami joined the Sangha and, we are told, eventually achieved Nirvana.

An even more poignant story, rivaling the trials of Job as a catalog of misfortunes, is told about a girl named Patachara. Patachara was the daughter of a rich man of Savatthi. Her parents were so possessive and protective toward her that they kept her confined in a room high up in their mansion. So, lacking companionship, she secretly fell in love with her page boy.

When she reached the age of sixteen Patachara's parents made arrangements for her to be married to the son of another rich man. Greatly distressed, she and her lover decided to elope and on the morning of the wedding day she disguised herself as a servant going to fetch water and slipped unnoticed out of the house. The lovers met at the edge of the city and went to a far place, where they got married.

In due course she became pregnant and as her time approached she recalled the custom whereby a woman should give birth to her child in her parents' house. She mentioned this to her husband, who was naturally horrified at the idea, but now her desire was so strong that she set out in spite of his objections. He followed, begging her to turn back, until in the middle of their journey she went into labor and gave birth. There was no point in going on and they returned home.

A second time she became pregnant and as before she set out for her parents' home, followed by her reluctant husband. But this time tragedy was to strike. Along the way a violent storm arose and at the same time Patachara began to feel birth pains. She settled down as well as she could, while her husband went off into the woods to get some branches and make a shelter for her. As he was cutting down a bush he was bitten by a snake and fell down dead. Troubles now came thick and fast. She bore her child and the three of them—she herself, her elder child and the baby spent the night exposed to the tempest and rain. The next day they came across the dead body of her husband. There was nothing to do but continue her journey, so carrying her baby on her hip and leading the other child by the hand Patachara walked on until she reached a swollen river. Not feeling strong enough to carry both children across at one time, Patachara left the older one on the bank while she took the baby across to the other side. No sooner had she put him down than a bird of prey swooped toward him. She shouted at the bird to scare it off, whereupon the boy on the other bank, thinking his mother was calling him, jumped into the river to join her. Horrified, Patachara herself plunged into the water to try and save him; but too late, he was swept away by the current and drowned. Meanwhile, before she could reach the bank the bird returned and made off with the baby.

> *"Words have the power to destroy or heal. When words are both true and kind, they can change our world."*

As if this was not sufficient calamity, a further shock awaited Patachara when she reached Savatthi. Anxious for news of her parents she stopped a man on the outskirts of the city and asked him if he knew them. "Ask me about any other family," he replied, and went on to tell how, the previous night, their house was destroyed by heavy rain— the same storm Patachara and her children had endured— and they had died in its collapse. The man pointed to a fire nearby which, he explained, was their funeral pyre.

It is worth remarking that, if such a tale of misery strains the credulity of the modern Western reader, disasters on this scale are still not uncommon in a part of the world regularly ravaged by floods or else parched by drought and always beset by natural dangers of one kind or another. Even so, it is difficult to imagine a sadder tale and it serves as a graphic and memorable parable to illustrate the Buddha's message.

On hearing that she had lost everything Patachara collapsed helpless with grief. While she lay weeping and writhing on the ground some people came by and took her to the Jetavana monastery where the Buddha was preaching. The Buddha asked some of the women present to wash and clothe her, and give her food, and then he began to talk to her about her misfortune. Taking refuge in his teaching she too joined the Sangha and eventually, we are told, gained Enlightenment.

From his childhood, when he had disputed with his cousin Devadatta over the wounded swan, Gautama is depicted as showing concern for all living things. Such compassion is perhaps the reverse side of the coin that bears on its face the motto "Sorrow is universal"; certainly in the course of the Buddha's teaching there are various examples of this charitable feeling in action.

On one occasion, while visiting a monastery with his attendant Ananda, the Buddha entered a room where a monk lay sick. He was suffering from diarrhea, and besides being in great pain, was in a filthy condition. No one, however, showed the least concern for him.

"Why are the other monks not attending you?" asked the Buddha.

"Because I do not attend them," he answered.

The Buddha called Ananda and together they began to minister to the sick monk. They boiled water and washed him, and then they moved him from his bed to a clean resting place. When they had finished the Buddha summoned the other monks and exhorted them to look after the sick and suffering.

"Whoever attends the sick attends me," he said.

On another occasion a monk at the Jetavana monastery developed a skin ailment that covered his body in boils. As the boils burst they caused terrible sores that stained his garments. His condition became so unpleasant that his fellow monks in desperation carried him out of the monastery and abandoned him on some open ground. Hearing of this the Buddha, again accompanied by Ananda, went out to tend to him. This time the other monks rallied to the Buddha's example and between them they prepared hot water, washed the monk's clothes and made him comfortable.

Stories are told, too, where the Buddha admonished children for being cruel to animals. In one instance he came across some boys amusing themselves at the expense of some fish trapped in an almost dry reservoir. Another time he found some boys attacking a snake with a stick.

The Buddha used these opportunities to explain the law of moral causation—that one is morally responsible for the consequences of one's acts, good or evil. But at the same time, being a practical man with an understanding of human psychology, he seems to have appealed to the better instincts of these children in much the same way as parents and teachers have always done when trying to restrain the unthinking brutality of youth. He asked them in effect: "How would you like somebody to do that to you?"

Practicality and common sense are fundamental to the teaching of the Buddha. They are what perhaps most obviously distinguishes Buddhism from the practice of others both then and now who renounce the worldly life— the ascetics, hermits, yogis and so on who had adopted "sanyas," or rigorous self-denial and withdrawal from ordinary human activity—and which Gautama had himself repudiated after following it for six years. Common sense is the foundation of the Middle Way, which essentially means avoiding such fanatical adherence to a particular course of action or attitude of mind that it can itself become an imprisonment, another kind of "clinging." Yet, because it is so difficult to define, the moderation taught by the Buddha has created difficulties for many of his followers, since those who adopt the religious life tend to do so with the zeal of total commitment and have little patience with measures.

This common sense of the Buddha—and, incidentally, his ordinary straightforward kindness—is illustrated in a touching story that echoes his own experiment with asceticism. One day the Buddha and his entourage were the guests of the inhabitants of a place called Alavi. One of those who had determined to go and hear him was a poor farmer, but on the morning of the visit one of his oxen was discovered missing. Torn between his desire to hear the Buddha and his concern for his ox, the farmer set out early to look for the animal, intending to join the meeting later. But by the time he had found the ox and returned it to the herd it was approaching evening. He had eaten nothing all day, but it was now so late that he could not delay further, so he went straight to the meeting.

Meanwhile the Buddha and his companions had been invited to a meal by the people of Alavi and the Buddha was about to "give thanks" in the customary way by preaching a sermon. At this point the farmer arrived. Seeing this poor man, looking so tired and weak, standing in front of him, the Buddha asked one of the stewards to find him a  place to sit and give him food. Only when the farmer had finished eating did the Buddha begin his discourse, to which the farmer listened with rapt attention.

Some of the monks with the Buddha raised their eyebrows at such concern for one man, especially a poor farmer who had arrived late, and after the meeting they began to grumble about what seemed to them the unorthodox behavior of their leader. Hearing these complaints, the Buddha explained: "If I had preached to this man while he was suffering the pangs of hunger he would not have been able to follow me. There is no affliction like the affliction of hunger."

But the Buddha also made it clear that in urging moderation he was not by any means condoning indulgence.

On the contrary, moderation implied restraint—restraint of all appetites, including that for self-punishment.

King Pasenadi of Kosala was a man who liked his food. A good meal for him meant boiled rice by the bucketful, with curries and sauces in corresponding measure. One day after breakfasting in his usual style he began to feel drowsy, but not wishing to fall asleep so early in the day he went for a walk to the Jetavana monastery where the Buddha was staying. With a weary look he flopped down near the Buddha, barely able to keep his eyes open.

"What is the matter, great King?" asked the Buddha. "Did you not sleep well?"

"Oh no, your reverence," he replied courteously. "I always have this trouble after eating."

"Great King," said the Buddha, "your trouble is from eating too much. Anyone who lives indolently, sleeping all the time and overeating so he rolls about like a hog fed on grain, is a fool, because that is bound to mean suffering."

Then the Buddha went on: "Great King, it is wise to observe moderation in food, because that way lies contentment. A man who is abstemious in eating will grow old slowly and will not have a lot of physical trouble and discomfort."

Poor Pasenadi, however, could not discipline himself, so the Buddha called the King's nephew, Prince Sudassana, and requested that he help. He told the prince the advice he had given to Pasenadi and asked him to watch the King whenever he had a meal. Whenever the King was about to seize the last handful of rice in his dish the prince should stop him and remind him of the Buddha's advice. Then for the King's next meal Sudassana should prepare only as much rice as had been left at the previous one. The King cooperated enthusiastically in this training—indeed, he even penalized his gluttony by giving away a thousand pieces of money in alms each time be had to be reminded of the Buddha's words—and soon he had reduced his consumption of rice to a modest potful a day. Transformed by this regime into a lean and energetic figure of a man, the King went to thank the Buddha.

"Now I am happy again," he said. "Once more I am able to go hunting and catch wild animals and horses. In the past I used to quarrel with my nephew, but now we are on such good terms that I have given him my own daughter in marriage. Then the other day a precious stone belonging to my household was lost; this has now been found and returned, to my great joy. Moreover, in order to create closer friendship with your community I have given the daughter of one of your kinsmen a place in my household, and that has caused me much pleasure."

King Pasenadi, the champion of the balanced diet, also figures in a story meant to illustrate balanced judgment. This serves to show, if nothing else, that moderation, common sense, restraint, these characteristics of the spiritually mature outlook, apply to all activities and should underlie everyone's whole personality; they are not merely a code of discipline. One day when visiting the Buddha, King Pasenadi saw a group of ascetics walking along the road. With proper reverence, the King got up and saluted them respectfully. Then when they had gone he turned to the Buddha and asked him: "Do you think there were among those ascetics any that could be considered saints?" To this somewhat naive question the Buddha first pointed out that such a judgment would be difficult for a man of the world to make, caught up as he is in the life of the passions and preoccupied with matters like property.

Then he went on:

"It is only by dealing thoroughly with a man, and over a long period, that you can know about his virtue. It is not something to be discovered by a moment's thought, nor can a fool learn it, only a wise man."

"It is by long association with a man that his integrity can be judged. It is in times of trouble that a man's fortitude becomes apparent. And it is in dealing with a man, conversing with him extensively, that one is able to tell how wise he is."

TEN

The Leaves in the Trees

The Buddha claimed no supernatural ability in evaluating his fellow men; his judgment was the fruit of experience, maturity and, above all, self-knowledge. The same balance characterized his attitude to praise and criticism, even when he himself was the subject.

Once the Buddha was on a journey with a company of monks. Traveling along the same road a little way behind were two ascetics, Suppiya and his pupil Brahmadatta, who belonged to a different school. As they walked, Suppiya and Brahmadatta were arguing about the Buddha, his doctrine and his Order. Suppiya was inclined to be critical, but Brahmadatta, with the enthusiasm of youth, was all praise. They stopped for the night at the same rest house as the Buddha and his followers, but their dispute continued, and some of the monks overheard it. Upset that they should be the subject of such comment these monks began to talk among themselves the following morning. Eventually the argument came to the Buddha's notice.

"My brothers," he said to them, "why are you unhappy and angry to hear people criticize me, or my doctrine or the Order? Such anger and unhappiness will only come in the way of your own self-conquest. If you get annoyed when others speak against you, how can you properly weigh the validity of what they say? When people talk critically about us you should examine what they say to find out what is not valid and then point it out, giving the reasons. Similarly, if anyone speaks approvingly of me, of my doctrine or of the Order, there is no cause to feel overjoyed. You should simply acknowledge whatever is correctly said and say why it is correct. After all, when people offer me praise, it is usually with regard to inessential matters, trivial aspects of behavior, not the things that are really important."

"As you walk and eat and travel, be where you are. Otherwise you will miss most of your life."

A tale with a similar theme is told about a zealous lay disciple called Atula. Atula, who had many friends, lived at Savatthi, and one day he suggested to his friends that they go to the monastery to listen to a discourse. They first encountered the monk Revata and, saluting him respectfully, sat down near him expecting he would address them. Revata, however, was a solitary, contemplative type, and had nothing to say to them.

Disappointed, they got up and went to see Sariputta, the famous exponent of the doctrine. Sariputta was only too glad to oblige them and launched into a lengthy and detailed discourse on philosophy. But this did not satisfy Atula and his friends either, for they found it abstruse and tedious.

They decided to try once more, and found themselves in the company of Ananda. They explained why they had come, and how they had not got what they wanted from either Revata or Sariputta. So Ananda attempted a compromise and gave them a brief discourse expressed in simple language. But still they were not content, and finally they went to complain to the Buddha. This is what he had to say:

"Throughout history it has been the practice of men to criticize other men. A man who says nothing is liable to be criticized, as is a man who says a great deal or a man who says neither too little nor too much. Everyone comes in for blame, as well as praise; even kings do. The great earth, the sun, the moon, I myself sitting and speaking in the assembly, are criticized by some and praised by others. But praise and blame bestowed idly are of no account. It is the praise or blame of the truly discerning man that matters."

Scholars love to argue over the philosophical implications of the Buddha's teachings. What did the Buddha really think, for instance, about the soul, which, according to classical Hindu belief, is a fragment of divinity in each individual seeking ultimately to be reabsorbed by the universal soul? Did the Buddha believe in an objective, external God? Can Buddhism indeed be truly called a religion?

The Buddha was certainly not averse to philosophic speculation and, as his career amply demonstrates, even allowing for legendary embellishment, he possessed a mind as agile as any of his time. Also, some sort of philosophical structure was necessary for his teaching if only to relate it to contemporary doctrines. But it emerges clearly from the accounts of his life that he regarded the value of such speculation as strictly limited and that he mistrusted it in general as potentially a distraction from the pursuit of the spiritual life. The core of his teaching is that, as everyone can see for himself, the human condition is rooted in suffering, but that with appropriate discipline and effort it is possible to achieve release from this suffering and discover a fulfilment beyond description in terms of ordinary human experience. When he speaks, as he often does, about the "Truth," he means this fulfilment, not a description or explanation of objective reality; indeed, implicit in the whole effort of seeking that experience is the conviction that, on its achievement, objective reality as it is generally understood will become irrelevant. This, it may well be argued, is begging the question, for how can one be confident about a method of procedure before putting the method to the  test? Such an objection would itself be condemned as irrelevant by the Buddha, since he would regard every minute or hour spent on pondering along such lines as so much delay in the process of gaining spiritual insight. We are here concerned with faith.

There are many stories and parables to illustrate the Buddha's impatience with philosophical argument. One concerns the monk Malunkyaputta.

Malunkyaputta had a restless mind and his meditation was constantly disturbed by universal questions to which he felt he was entitled to have an answer from the Buddha. But every time he raised them, the Buddha shrugged them off without a satisfactory explanation. Finally he could stand the uncertainty no longer and went to the Buddha with an ultimatum: either he received a proper reply or he left the Order and returned to lay life. He then pedantically spelled out the problems that were troubling him. Is the universe eternal or not? Is the universe finite or infinite? Is the soul identical with the body or are they separate? And so on.

"You have failed to give me answers to these questions, and this upsets me," he said. "If the Blessed One will explain these matters to me I will continue to follow the holy life under him, but if not I will leave the Order and go away. After all, if the Blessed One knows that the universe is eternal, why not say so; if he does not know, well then it is quite in order to admit it straightforwardly and say 'I don't know.'"

The Buddha first admonished Malunkyaputta for attempting to blackmail him. "Did I ever say to you: 'Come, Malunkyaputta, lead the holy life under me and I will make plain such matters to you'?" he asked. He then went on to tell Malunkyaputta a parable.

"Imagine a man who is struck by a poisoned arrow. His friends and relatives rush him to a surgeon, but before they do anything the man says: 'I will not let this arrow be removed until I know who was the man who shot me; whether he belongs to the Kshatriya or Brahmin or Vaishya or Sudra caste; what are his name and clan; whether he is tall, short or of medium height; whether he is dark in complexion or brown or yellowish; from which village or town he comes. And I must know what kind of bow was used to shoot the arrow; what sort of bowstring was used;

the type of arrow; the kind of feather that was used on the arrow and with what the arrow was tipped.'

"Malunkyaputta, that man would die before he could know any of these things. The same is the case of anyone who says he will not devote himself to the holy life until he knows the answer to such questions as whether the universe is eternal and finite."

The Buddha went on to explain that the holy life does not depend on such questions. Whatever conclusion one may reach about them, the essential facts of life remain—birth, old age, decay, death, sorrow, pain, lamentation and "the cessation of these things that I declare to be possible in this life."

"Therefore, Malunkyaputta, accept whatever I have explained and do not concern yourself with what I have not explained. Those questions that you raise, why have I not attempted to give you an answer? Because they are not of any use or relevance to the spiritual life. They do not help you to achieve detachment, tranquillity, deep realization and ultimately Nirvana. What have I told you about? I have told you about unhappiness, the cessation of unhappiness and the way to bring about that cessation. And I have told you about these because they are fundamental to the spiritual life."

In a similar vein, the Buddha once began talking to some of his monks while they were sitting in a grove of simsapa trees. Gathering up a few simsapa leaves in his hand the Buddha said to the monks: "Which are more numerous, the leaves in my hand or those in the trees overhead?"

"There are far more in the trees," replied the monks.

"Such is the comparison between the truths I have realized and revealed to you and those that I have not revealed," said the Buddha. "Those things that I have not revealed are not useful to the pure life and do not assist your spiritual progress. What I have revealed is the nature of unhappiness and how to overcome it, for these are truths that lead to Nirvana."

Not surprisingly, the Buddha also had little patience with dogmatism. If philosophical speculation is essentially futile, how much more so is preoccupation with theological dogma. This attitude is amusingly demonstrated in one of the best-known stories relating to the Buddha, a story that has probably been heard by many people in one form or another even if they do not connect it with Buddhism.

On one occasion a number of ascetics and learned men were gathered at Savatthi, while the Buddha was residing there. They began to discuss philosophical matters and soon they were busily debating the same sort of questions as those that had so agitated Malunkyaputta—whether the world is eternal and infinite, whether body and soul are separate, whether perfection is attainable during life, and so on. The argument became so heated that it moved from the academic level to one of personal abuse. Eventually the Buddha was summoned to intervene, and he dealt with the situation by telling the following parable.

There was once a king who, seeking some entertainment for himself, had a number of people who had been blind since birth brought together in front of him. An elephant was then led in and made to stand in the midst of them, and they were instructed to reach out so as to feel the part of the animal nearest them. Accordingly some felt its head, some an ear, some a tusk, while others felt its trunk or its foot or its tail, and one felt the tuft on the end of its tail. The king then asked the blind men in turn to say what they thought an elephant resembled. Those who had felt its ample, hard head said: "An elephant is like a cooking pot." Those who had felt an ear said: "Like a basket for winnowing grain." A tusk suggested a ploughshare, the trunk the shaft of a plough, a leg a pillar, the tail a pestle, while the man who had felt only the tuft of the tail said: "An elephant is like a broom." A great argument developed among the holders of these varying opinions and before long they came to blows, to the huge

> *"What has long been neglected cannot be restored immediately. Fruit falls from the tree when it is ripe. The way cannot be forced."*

amusement of the king. Such, explained the Buddha, is the case of people who have seen one aspect of reality and then dogmatically suppose that they have seen the whole reality.

An elephant simile is used by the Buddha in another parable in which patience and humility are recommended in the pursuit of truth. An ordinary, unskilled man goes into a forest and sees a large footprint. That, he says to himself, must be the footprint of the great royal elephant. But the skilled tracker who sees the print is more cautious. Such a footprint could have been made by a stunted cow elephant treading heavily. The tracker looks around for other evidence. He sees that branches high up have been broken off by the elephant's shoulders. He still does not assume, however, that the great royal elephant was responsible until he has found enough additional evidence to satisfy all his doubts. Only then does he say: "Yes, this is the footprint of the great royal elephant itself."

Similarly, said the Buddha, spiritual progress is achieved in stages and one should not allow oneself to think that perfection has been achieved at any stage while it is possible to persevere further.

ELEVEN

The Inner Life

Buddhism is not for those who like to be told how to order their lives, who look constantly for guidance to an outside authority, whether in the form of priest, scripture or ritual. Throughout the Buddha's teaching, along with his insistence on balance and common sense, there is an implied obligation on each individual to think things out for himself, to make up his own mind and make his own moral decisions. Naturally there has to be a framework, and this the Buddha provides with the eightfold path. But the doctrine of karma requires each man ultimately to be responsible for his own salvation; it is no use looking for an insurance policy either in observance of safe formulas or in total inactivity.

On one occasion the Buddha visited the town of Kesaputta, which seems to have been a popular spot for ascetics and religious teachers. The local people, known as Kalamas, were perplexed because each teacher who came to talk to them expounded his own particular doctrine and tore to shreds the doctrines of everybody else. When the Buddha arrived they approached him with the challenging question: "How are we to tell which of all these learned men who address us is telling us the truth?"

The Buddha replied: "You are quite right to feel doubts and uncertainty. In making up your minds about the validity of a doctrine do not rely only on what you have heard said about it, upon reputation or upon rumors; nor should you depend on scriptures, or axioms or specious reasoning, nor upon the seeming cleverness of the teacher, nor should you simply assume that because a man is an ascetic he is a worthy teacher. You have to know inside yourselves what things are bad, what things would be censured by a wise man and which, if pursued, would lead to harm and ill."

Some will object that this again is begging the question and, like the Kalamas, demand some absolute standard of judgment. Certainly the extent of sectarianism and intolerance in the world does not seem to have diminished in the two and a half millennia since the Buddha answered the Kalamas. But the Buddha's reply to such an objection would be to direct attention inward, to the human factors of desire, anger, delusion and so on which impede the exercise of sound judgment, and this was indeed what he did with the Kalamas, reportedly to their eventual satisfaction.

It goes without saying that for the Buddha to allow any kind of personality cult to develop around him would have been quite inconsistent with the spirit of his teaching. Nevertheless, since respect and reverence, particularly in the religious context, can easily lead to hero-worship and even deification, the Buddha is at pains on a number of occasions to stress that what matters is his teaching, not himself as an individual.

While traveling near Rajagaha at what must have been an early stage in his missionary career, the Buddha stopped for overnight shelter in a potter's shed. Also spending the night was a young recluse, and the Buddha began talking to him. "Of which teacher are you a follower?" he began, since those who took up the holy life generally identified themselves with one school or another.

Not knowing who the other man was, the young man, by name Pukkusati, replied: "There is a recluse called Gautama, a scion of the Sakya royal family who left his home for the religious life. He is very well spoken of and it is said he is a saint, a fully enlightened one. It is in his name that I have decided to become a recluse, and I regard him as my master and his doctrine as the one I wish to follow."

"Have you ever seen him, this Enlightened One? Would recognize him if you saw him?" asked the Buddha.

"No, I have never seen him, and I should not recognize if I saw him." said Pukkusati.

Thereupon the Buddha, without revealing who he was, offered to explain his doctrine, and the young man readily agreed. Only toward the end of the discourse did Pukkusati begin to realize that it was being delivered by the Buddha himself and when it was over he bowed to his master, apologizing for not knowing him and asking to be ordained into the Sangha.

In order to be ordained, Pukkusati needed to have an alms bowl and robes, but while he was out trying to obtain these he was attacked by a cow and killed. When the Buddha heard this he praised Pukkusati as a wise man who had grasped the truth and who had been sincerely concerned with the doctrine rather than the teacher.

A story with a similar moral is told about a young man of Savatthi named Vakkali. The Buddha spent much of his time in Savatthi and seeing him coming and going in the town Vakkali developed what can only be described as an infatuation for him. Whenever he saw the Buddha he was overcome with admiration. One day Vakkali said to himself: "As long as I remain living at home I cannot see the Buddha as often as I should like, so I had better go to the monastery and become a monk. Then I can see him every day." Duly he went to the monastery and was ordained.

Vakkali was now able to admire the Buddha as much as he wanted and followed him like a shadow, gazing at him with unvarying adulation. The Buddha was aware of this but said nothing, preferring to wait until Vakkali was a little older. After a few years, when he thought he had matured sufficiently, the Buddha said to Vakkali: "Vakkali, what is the use of gazing all the time at my body, which is something transient and impermanent? If you really want to see me, look at my teaching."

However, this had no effect, so the Buddha decided to be firm. One day he was invited to go for three months to Rajagaha, and when Vakkali got up to go with him he told him: "No, Vakkali, you cannot come with me. I have to go alone."

Deeply disappointed, Vakkali returned to his cell and began to wonder how he could pass three months without seeing his hero. He decided he could not, and climbed to the top of a mountain with the intention of throwing himself to his death. At this point the Buddha miraculously appeared to him to explain that only through his teaching could happiness be achieved, and Vakkali at last realized the folly of his ways.

There is nothing academic about the Buddha's moral teaching; it is firmly rooted in experience of human nature and it was regularly put to the test during his leadership of the Sangha. Monks, it would seem, are no less liable to jealousy, quarreling and petty-mindedness than anyone else. Dealing with the tensions that arose within the Sangha must have been one of the Buddha's more common tasks, and on at least one occasion it appears he became thoroughly disgusted by the behavior of his followers.

A dispute over a small matter concerning the rules of hygiene broke out at a monastery in Kosambi between two senior members of the Order, one a leading exponent of the Doctrine, the other a specialist in the Discipline. The issue was taken up by the respective pupils of these two men and soon it grew into an open quarrel involving other monks, nuns, lay supporters and even some people who were not followers of the Buddha at all. At one stage the Discipline man pronounced excommunication against the Doctrine man for allegedly refusing to acknowledge his original breach of the hygiene rules. The Buddha sent a message to the Kosambi monastery asking the monks to stop quarreling, and when that did not work he went there in person. But still they would not listen, so, disheartened, the Buddha went away. He wan-

dered off alone, and settled down for the rainy season in a forest called Parileyya, where he was befriended by an elephant.

Hearing that the Buddha had abandoned the monks to their squabbling, the lay Buddhists of Kosambi withdrew their support from the monks. This brought the monks to their senses and they hastily apologized to the lay supporters. The latter, however, refused to accept any apology until the monks had made their peace with the Buddha, and as it was now the rainy season they could not go in search of him. They then spent the next few weeks in some misery.

> *"Take time every day to sit quietly and listen."*

The description of the Buddha's stay in Parileyya forest contrasts sharply with the discord experienced by his followers in Kosambi. The elephant not only protected the Buddha from the danger of wild animals but went with him to beg for alms, carrying his bowl and robe on his head. One day a monkey added his services to that of the elephant by collecting some wild honey and giving it to the Buddha to eat. This was an idyllic period showing the Buddha in harmony with nature.

Meanwhile, it became known that the Buddha was staying in the forest, attended by a noble elephant, and in the city of Savatthi some of the leading figures, including Anathapindaka, approached Ananda and asked him to persuade the Buddha to return so that the trouble with the monks at Kosambi could be resolved. Accompanied by a large number of monks, Ananda went to the forest. The Buddha greeted them with the somewhat bitter words: "When one has intelligent companions worth associating with, who lead a good life, then one should live with them happily and cooperatively. Otherwise live alone like a king who has abandoned his kingdom, or an elephant in the forest. There is no companionship with a fool; it is better to be alone."

Nevertheless, he agreed to return with them to Savatthi. The parting with the elephant, incidentally, is portrayed as a poignant scene, with the animal weeping bitterly. When the Buddha was back in the Jetavana monastery, at Savatthi, the Kosambi monks came to beg his pardon. By this time, however, they were thoroughly unpopular. The King of Kosala threatened not to allow them into his territory, and Anathapindaka was reluctant to let them enter the Jetavana monastery. When the monks finally did arrive they were given separate lodgings, and were treated with overt contempt by the other monks. But the Buddha himself showed no vindictiveness. "These monks are good people," he told the King of Kosala and Anathapindaka. "It is only because of a dispute among themselves that they paid no attention to my words." When they came before him, ashamed and contrite, and threw themselves at his feet, the Buddha admonished them and then gave them a simple lesson: "Some people do not realize that quarrels will fade away by themselves. If you know this you will cease to have dissension."

Perhaps the most dramatic example of the Buddha's principles coming face to face with human reality is the occasion when he prevented a war. The Sakyans and the Koliyans were neighbors separated by the river Rohini, and jointly they dammed the river in order to irrigate their fields on each side. In the month of June, however, at the hottest time of the year, the river was running low and the crops began to droop. The Koliyans began to talk of diverting the water to their exclusive use, since there would not be enough for both of them, but the Sakyans would have none of this. Tempers rose and abuse was exchanged. One or two people came to blows, and eventually the two parties brought out their armies.

At this stage the Buddha came to know about the argument. It was a particularly delicate situation for him to become involved in since he was related to both clans— being the son of a Sakyan king and a Koliyan princess— but he saw it as his duty to intervene. There is an ironical comment on the nature of warmongering, how it comes to take on its own momentum regardless of the original reason, in the story of how he approached the site of the dispute and asked his kinsmen what all the trouble was about; no one of any rank was able to tell him what the quarrel was really about until he asked some of the slave laborers—the people lowest in the hierarchy—who told him "Water." The Buddha then went to the King and asked: "How much is water worth, great King?" "Very little," replied the King. "And how much are the lives of your people worth," the Buddha continued. "Oh, they are beyond price," said the King. "Well," said the Buddha, "is it right that for the sake of a little water you should destroy so many lives that are beyond price?"

> "Forgiveness is primarily for our own sake, so that we no longer carry the burden of resentment. But to forgive does not mean we will allow injustice again."

The Buddha then went on to address both sides as follows: "Great Kings, why do you act in this way? Were I not here today you would have started a river of blood flowing. You live in enmity and hatred. I live free from hatred. You live afflicted with the sickness of evil passions. I live free from such disease. You spend your lives in eager pursuit of sensual pleasures, whereas I do not. If we want to live happily, let us live without hate among men who hate. Let us live in good health among those who are sick. Let us live free from care among those who are careworn."

TWELVE

Nirvana

The Buddha carried out his ministry for forty-five years. The first intimation that he could not continue for much longer came while he was visiting the village of Beluva to spend the rainy season. During his stay there he fell ill, and began to suffer severe pain. He bore the pain uncomplainingly, but he thought to himself: "It is not right for me to pass away and finally attain Nirvana until I have spoken to my attendants and taken leave of the Sangha." So by force of will he fought the illness and found the strength to go on.

Then the Buddha summoned Ananda and said to him: "Ananda, what does the Sangha need from me? The Law I have taught is clear, there is no secret version of it distinct from the one I have explained; I have not kept a closed fist on anything. Now I am old, Ananda, I am past eighty. So, Ananda, let each of you make a refuge for himself, an island; and let that refuge be the Law and nothing else."

Their retreat ended, the Community once more set out and in due course came to a mango grove belonging to a man named Chunda. On learning that the Buddha was present, Chunda went so see him, and after hearing instruction from him, invited the Community to take food with him the next day. The following morning the Buddha went with his followers to Chunda's house, where they were served a rich meal that included mushrooms. It was after, and perhaps because of, this meal that the Buddha's sickness returned. This time there was to be no recovery.

Despite his illness, the Buddha went on his way, coming eventually to a place called Kusinara. Here he settled in a grove of sala trees on the bank of the river Hirannavati. Ananda prepared a couch for him between two sala trees and the Buddha lay down. Then, addressing Ananda, he again made the point that it was not he himself, but what he said, that mattered. "It may be, Ananda," he said, "that in some of you the thought will arise 'the word of the Master is ended; we have no teacher any more.' But that is not the way to look at it, Ananda. The Law that I have explained and laid down for you all, let that, after I am gone, be your teacher."

The Buddha then addressed the monks around him. "It is in the nature of all things that take form to dissolve again. Strive earnestly (to attain perfection)." These were the last words of the Buddha who then, it is said, moved through various rapturous stages of meditation until he passed away. His remains were cremated with the honors due to a royal person.

Notwithstanding all they had learned about the transience of life, some of the monks began to mourn bitterly the passing of their teacher. There was one present, however, who took quite a different attitude. This was the monk Subhadda who had entered the Sangha in his old age, and for him the death of the Buddha was a relief. "Enough, friends, do not be sorrowful," he said. "Do not lament, we are well rid of the Great Monk. We have been frustrated by his saying 'you may do this, you may not do that.' Now we can do as we like, and not do those things we do not want to do."

This, of course, was a signal for the Buddha's discipline to be abandoned, and for the Sangha to break up in confusion. So it was interpreted by one of the senior monks, the great Kassapa of Uruvela, who decided that a full and authentic record of the Buddha's teaching must be established as quickly as possible. Accordingly, an assembly was arranged in the city of Rajagaha, with the blessing of King Ajatasattu, and 500 monks who had attained saint-

hood were summoned
to attend. With Kas-
sapa presiding, this
Council rehearsed and
committed to memory
all that was known
about the Buddha's
teaching. Upali and

Ananda played leading parts in formulating respectively,
under the interrogation of Kassapa, the Discipline and
the Discourses. The Council lasted seven months.

The material produced at this Council was only
committed to writing at the fourth Council held in Cey-
lon in about 80 BC. The Buddha's sayings and teachings
were divided into three sections which became known as
the "Tipitaka" or "three baskets of the Canon." These are
the *Vinaya*—the disciplinary rules for the Sangha; the
Sutta—the discourses given by the Buddha on different
occasions; the *Abhidhamma*—the philosophical and psycho-
logical development of the teaching that was formally
closed only at the third Council in about 246 BC.

It is important to appreciate the nature of the texts
that have come down to us, particularly the discourses in
the *Sutta* section. Originally, it was intended that each of
these discourses—which consist of terse sayings of either
the Buddha or one of his leading disciples—should be

memorized, probably due to lack of durable writing materials. For this reason the device of repeating key phrases was instituted in order to make the task easier. The reader may recall that the tradition of oral transmission was followed by other Indian contemporaries of the Buddha as well as by teachers in China and Greece at that time.

It is the Tipitaka that has provided the basis for this little book.

Photo credits:

pages viii, 8, 24, 105: Tibetan tanka depicting the life of the Buddha. 18th century. Guimet Museum of Asian Art, Paris, France. Photo RMN-Arnaudet

page 23: Skull, wall-painting from Qizil, *c.* A.D. 500

page 33: Siddhartha as ascetic. Gandhara sculpture. 2nd century A.D. Lahore Museum, India

page 42: Gandharan frieze depicting Buddha's first sermon. Late 2nd–early 3rd century. Courtesy of the Freer Gallery of Art, Smithsonian Institution, Washington, D.C.

page 52: Gandharan frieze showing Buddha's enlightenment. Late 2nd–early 3rd century. Courtesy of the Freer Gallery of Art, Smithsonian Institution, Washington, D.C.

page 65: Novice monk with begging bowl, marble statuette. 19th century. British Museum, London

pages 91, 97, 110, 117: Tibetan tanka depicting the Three Jewels. 19th century. Museum für Völkerkunde, Munich. Photograph by Autrum-Mulzer

page 125: Gandharan frieze showing Buddha's death. Late 2nd–early 3rd century. Courtesy of the Freer Gallery of Art, Smithsonian Institution, Washington, D.C.

Venerable Dr. Hammalawa Saddhatissa, the author of *Buddhist Ethics* and *The Buddha's Way*, was an ordained Buddhist monk. He studied at the universities of Benares, London and Edinburgh and was a professor of Buddhism. Dr. Saddhatissa was also head of the London Buddhist Vihara and served as president of the British Mahabodhi Society and the Sangha Council.

Jack Kornfield was trained as a Buddhist monk in Burma, Thailand, and India beginning in the 1960s. Since that time he has been instrumental in making Buddhist practice accessible to Westerners as a teacher, writer and co-founder of meditation centers. Among his bestselling books are *A Path with Heart*, *Soul Food*, *Buddha's Little Instruction Book*, and *A Still Forest Pool*.

OTHER SEASTONE TITLES

WHAT WOULD BUDDHA DO?:
101 ANSWERS TO LIFE'S DAILY DILEMMAS
Franz Metcalf

Much as the "WWJD?" books help Christians live better lives by drawing on the wisdom of Jesus, this "WWBD?" book provides advice on improving your life by following the wisdom of another great teacher—Buddha. Not just for Buddhists, *WWBD?* is for anyone looking for spiritual direction and help in navigating through contemporary society. *Hardcover. $15.00*

THE TAO OF THE JUMP SHOT:
AN EASTERN APPROACH TO LIFE AND BASKETBALL
John Fitzsimmons Mahoney   Introduction by Bill Walton

Much more than a book about basketball, *The Tao of the Jump Shot* describes how to move with grace, prize every action and experience the beauty of life through the simple act of getting a ball through a hoop. *Trade paper. $9.95*

JESUS AND BUDDHA: THE PARALLEL SAYINGS
Marcus Borg, Editor   Introduction by Jack Kornfield

Traces the life stories and beliefs of Jesus and Buddha, then presents a comprehensive collection of their remarkably similar teachings on facing pages. *Trade paper. $14.00*

JESUS AND LAO TZU: THE PARALLEL SAYINGS
Martin Aronson

Comparing the New Testament with the Tao Te Ching, Taoism's most sacred book, *Jesus and Lao Tzu: The Parallel Sayings* features an astonishing series of examples in which these two spiritual masters lead their followers down the same path in spite of differences in time and geography. *Hardcover. $19.00*

THE SACRED EAST: AN ILLUSTRATED GUIDE TO BUDDHISM, HINDUISM, CONFUCIANISM, TAOISM AND SHINTO
C. Scott Littleton, General Editor

The Sacred East illuminates the main philosophies and religions of Asia, exploring the Hindu traditions of India, the richly varied Buddhist faith, the Confucian and Taoist beliefs of China and the Shinto religion of Japan. *Trade paper. $17.95*

SEX AND SPIRIT: AN ILLUSTRATED GUIDE
TO SACRED SEXUALITY
Clifford Bishop
Drawing on a range of traditions and cultures, this book traces the sexual act
throughout history and shows how entwined our sexuality is with out per-
sonal search for meaning and fulfillment. *Trade paper. $16.95*

MUSIC OF SILENCE
David Steindl-Rast with Sharon Lebell
Introduction by Kathleen Norris
A noted Benedictine monk shows us how to incorporate the sacred meaning
of monastic life into our everyday world by paying attention to the "seasons
of the day" and the enlivening messages to be found in each moment. *Trade
paper. $12.00*

THE GOSPEL OF THOMAS:
UNEARTHING THE LOST WORDS OF JESUS
John Dart and Ray Riegert   Introduction by John Dominic Crossan
Details the discovery of the greatest collection of apocryphal Christian doc-
uments ever found. The dramatic narrative history is combined with an
annotated translation of The Gospel of Thomas. *Trade paper. $12.00*

WHAT WOULD SHAKESPEARE DO?: PERSONAL ADVICE FROM
THE BARD
Jess Winfield
In a friendly, straightforward fashion, *What Would Shakespeare Do?* uncovers for
us all the personal advice contained in the Bard's immortal words. *WWSD?*
explores ideas that still resonate today: sex and love, youth and aging, morals
and the meaning of life. *Hardcover. $16.00*

*To order these titles or other Seastone books call 800-377-2542 or 510-601-8301,
e-mail ulysses@ulyssespress.com or write to Ulysses Press, P.O. Box 3440, Berkeley, CA
94703. There is no charge for shipping on retail orders. California residents must include
sales tax. Allow two to three weeks for delivery. Visit us at our website: ulyssespress.com.*